WINE
aficionado

WINE
aficionado

Janice Fuhrman

MQP

Published by MQ Publications Limited
12 The Ivories, 6–8 Northampton Street
London N1 2HY
tel: 020 7359 2244
fax: 020 7359 1616
email: mail@mqpublications.com
website: www.mqpublications.com

ISBN: 1-84072-966-X

1 3 5 7 9 0 8 6 4 2

Printed in China

This book contains the opinions and ideas of the author. It is
intended to provide helpful and informative material on the
subjects addressed in this book and is sold with the understanding
that the author and publisher are not engaged in rendering
medical, health, or any other kind of personal professional services
in this book. The reader should consult his or her medical, health,
or competent professional before adopting any of the suggestions
in this book or drawing references from it. The author and
publisher disclaim all responsibility for any liability, loss, or risk,
personal or otherwise, which is incurred as a consequence, directly
or indirectly, of the use and application of any of the contents of
this book.

CONTENTS

Introduction

I'm a California-based wine writer with an irresistible desire to share my passion, thoughts, experiences, ideas, and advice about wine with my readers. While it's true that I'm a wine "insider," you might also detect an underlying subversive note here. That's because my real aim is to demystify wine lore. Let's put it simply: do you believe you have to be educated about every aspect of chocolate or cheese to enjoy them? Of course not. And it's not necessary with wine.

It's still widely assumed that we need special expertise to appreciate wine, and become an "aficionado"—but in fact it's just one of many beverages we drink. Wine can be simple or it can be complex, well-crafted or mediocre, but at its core the experience of tasting and enjoying it is subjective—everyone experiences it in a unique way.

In *Wine Aficionado* no one is dictating which wines you should drink, or how, when, or why you should enjoy wine. On the contrary, what you'll find here is a direct, useful, clear guide to all the information and terminology you will encounter at the wine store, in wine magazines, on wine labels and at restaurants. This way, anyone—including you—can become a genuine wine aficionado, simply by being guided toward your own discoveries.

Here you'll find short, informative pointers covering everything you need to know about wine—there's something to discover on every page. *Wine Aficionado* is wonderfully user-friendly, too—feel free to dip straight into any section that interests you, and go directly to what you want to know. So, now you're all set to explore the joys of wine, why not pull up a chair, pop a cork, pour yourself a delicious glass, and read these encouraging tips to get you started?

- Relax about wine! It's about pleasure, not a contest to see who knows most.

- Banish all fear. Dare to ask for a wine that you don't know how to pronounce. It's the only way you will learn to taste something new. Be brave!

- Rely on help. Wine merchants, restaurant servers, *sommeliers,* even grocery-store clerks, all know something about the products they sell and serve, so ask them for help.

- Loosen up about the rules and let taste be your guide. Yes, there are lots of different tastes—but the most important is that you choose what seems good to you.

- Benefit from the fact that there are so many wine regions around the world turning out quantities of good-to-excellent wines. Competition among wine producers is at an all-time high.

- Learn the few rules necessary to store wine well, whether you have two bottles or two hundred.

- Enhance your wine with food and your food with wine. Wine is a perfectly natural companion for food, and increases its pleasure.

- Drink locally. When you travel, try the local wines and brews. They have evolved with the local cuisine and are usually uniquely suited to it.

See? It's not that difficult. All you need is an open mind, and a willingness to try all kinds of wines—that's the attitude that turns you into a real wine aficionado.

Janus Johnson

getting to

1

know wine

There's something about the subject of wine that seems to scare people. But you really don't have to be nervous. If someone tells you that there is such a thing as a "perfect" wine, that's just a personal opinion. There are fine wines, sweet wines, dry wines, and sparkling wines, but how good a particular bottle is remains a matter of subjective taste. You either like the flavor of the wine, or you don't. Essentially, the first step in feeling comfortable with wine is defining what you like and finding the particular wines that suit your taste. As you explore, you'll ask yourself lots of questions. Is it wrong to prefer sweet wines to dry? Is red wine better than white? Does it matter if you drink sweet wine with a main course? All this uncertainty will diminish when you begin to regard wine more as a familiar beverage rather than as a degree subject in gourmet expertise. Wine is simply a beverage to be enjoyed—and what you prefer to drink is entirely up to you.

Enjoying the heritage of wine

Wine has memorably been described as "bottled poetry"—and it is surely one of the greatest sources of pleasure that human beings have devised. It's no ordinary beverage, but something mysterious, complex, thought provoking, and wonderful that springs from something quite ordinary—the grape. Wine has been part of our living experience for five thousand years, inspiring the muses, fueling fellowship, and adding to our enjoyment of life. Agriculture, science, and art are all called upon in the making of this magical potion. Special wine grapes, a new vintage each year, are grown, harvested, pressed into wine, aged, and bottled. So, at one level, while wine is simply fermented grape juice, at another, it has become a great art form over thousands of years, a nectar that nourishes the dreams, festive occasions, and important milestones of life.

Get out there and explore

To take part fully in the great adventure that wine offers, you should always be positive in your approach to tasting new wines, and be willing to explore the wide selection of types that are available. You'll invariably find something that suits your taste, and the road to discovery will bring you great pleasure in itself. The more open-minded you are, the more confident you'll become. It's tempting to get stuck in a rut, and cling to the security of choosing the same familiar wine because it feels "safe." Fine, but then you're missing out on all the wonderful and varied delights that are out there waiting to be enjoyed. And if a particular wine is not to your taste, so what? Don't let that put you off. Move on, and try something else. There are so many types of wine to discover—all those wonderful reds, rosés, and whites, still and sparkling wines, ports and sherries—that you'll have lots of fun experimenting.

Start with the grape

It helps to acquire some basic knowledge about wine; apart from being useful in itself, it will give you more confidence. For instance, many people think that wine grapes are the same as the ones we eat. Not true. In fact, around 99.9 percent of wine grapes belong to a sub-genus called *Vitis vinifera*. Most wine grapes originated in Europe and central Asia and have been imported to other wine regions of the world. They are usually smaller than table grapes and always contain seeds. Although wine grapes are grown around the world on almost every continent, different grape varieties benefit from variations in soil type and climate.

What is terroir?

You may hear wine savvy people talk about *terroir*. This is a concept that originated in France and refers to the specific environment of a vineyard where grapes are grown. Factors such as altitude, slope, type of soil, drainage conditions, exposure to the sun, and microclimate all play a part in terroir. It is a powerful philosophy of wine-growing that elevates the land above winemaking techniques and the technology of the winery. Some in the wine industry argue against the importance of terroir, but it does help explain why even neighboring vineyards under the same management can produce wines of distinctly different styles and quality.

The range of wine styles

The reason wine is never boring is because winemakers make it in so many ways, using different grapes and methods to create still and sparkling wines in red, white, and rosé. One winemaker might create a style of wine that is lush, full-bodied, and unctuous, while another produces wine that is crisp, clean, and light. Wine can have a low or high alcohol content, and a low or high price tag. It can show off the flavors of the grape or get its character from other added flavors, such as oak from the barrels it is aged in, or from herbs or other fruit additives. Today, wine is so available and affordable that anyone can drink it—and no one needs superior knowledge to enjoy it. Cheers!

Red wine

Choose a red wine if you prefer a richer, weightier wine with deeper flavors. Reds are made from special red or "black" grapes, such as Cabernet Sauvignon, Merlot, Pinot Noir, or Zinfandel. The deep colors and flavors of most red wines result from the grape skins and seeds soaking together with the grape juice for days or weeks, and from aging in oak barrels. Tannins, found to a much greater degree in red wines than whites, give red wine its astringent quality and allow for bottles to age long into the future. Although most red wines can be enjoyed right away, some—usually the more expensive ones—will improve with age. If properly stored, most Pinot Noir and Zinfandel will improve in five to ten years and Cabernet Sauvignon will continue to improve ten to fifteen years after the date on the bottle.

White wine

It's called white wine because it's made from white (well, okay, green) grapes. Chardonnay, Sauvignon Blanc, Pinot Grigio, and Riesling are among the world's most popular white grape varieties. After the grapes are pressed to collect their juices, they are not fermented in contact with their skins the way red wines are. One exception to this is *blanc de noirs*, a white or lightly tinted Champagne made from the juice of black grapes. If there is a tint to the wine, it comes from pigments in the grape skins, but the skins are removed before the wine turns a deeper color. White wines are usually lighter, fresher, and more delicate than reds, and are a good place to start if you're new to drinking wine. White wines can be aged in oak barrels for a richer, fuller-bodied wine, as is often done with "New World" Chardonnay (e.g. from California and Australia). Or they might be aged in large, stainless-steel tanks, giving a crisp, clean profile to the wine.

Rosé wine

Most rosé wines are made from red or black grapes in much the same way red wines are, except their skins are allowed to soak with the grape juice for only a short time—just enough to tint the juice a pink or light red color. Dry rosé wines are often made from Pinot Noir, Cabernet Franc, and other red grape varieties. And sweeter versions, usually called "blush wines" in the U.S., are often made from the Zinfandel or Merlot grape and sold as "White Zinfandel" or "White Merlot." Rosés or blush wines are not for aging, but for drinking young. As with white wines, serve rosé wines well-chilled. They are most popular in the summer, but if you like them, there is no reason not to drink them all year round. Rosé is known as *rosado* in Spain and *rosato* in Italy.

Champagne

The tiny bubbles in Champagne or sparkling wine are produced from putting the wine through two fermentations, the second one taking place in the bottle. Often reserved for celebrations such as weddings, anniversaries, and New Year's Eve, Champagne is a festive drink, but it also goes with any meal at any time of year. Its name comes from the specific region of France where the classic method of making Champagne, known as *méthode champenoise*, originated (see page 122). Although there are several other, less expensive, ways of putting bubbles in wine, *méthode champenoise* is widely considered to be the highest-quality wine.

Sparkling wine

It's easy to be confused by the range of names used for "Champagne." There's sparkling wine in the U.S., cava in Spain, Sekt in Germany, and Prosecco and Asti in Italy. Then, of course, there's French Champagne. Most high-end American producers of Champagnes call their products "sparkling wine" to differentiate them from the wines made in the Champagne region of France, but they are usually made using the same French method. The Spanish sparkling wine known as cava is mostly made using the *méthode champenoise*, although with very different grape varieties. Cava costs less than French Champagne and is a great substitute when it's your friend's birthday and you want to be festive, but can't afford the real thing. Champagne is best when served cold. While you are enjoying your first glasses, keep the bottle chilled in an ice bucket or return it to the refrigerator until you need a refill.

Aperitifs

If you're having folks over for dinner, why not welcome them with a glass of wine that is specially designed to enjoy before eating? These are known as aperitifs, and are meant for drinking in relatively small amounts before a meal to whet the appetite for the feast to come. There's plenty of choice—a glass of light white wine, Champagne, a kir or kir royale, or perhaps fortified wines such as sherry, Dubonnet, (laced with herbs and quinine), or vermouth, a fortified wine flavored with spices, herbs and fruits. All are popularly served as aperitifs.

Sherry

Sherry is *the* aperitif in Spain. It's perfect for the typical Spanish eating style, where you may not sit down to dinner until close to midnight, after snacking during the day on *tapas*—nibbles of olives, anchovies, fried peppers, salted almonds, squid—and glasses of chilled *fino*. It originated in the Jerez de la Frontera area, and is enjoyed around the world. Sherry is made by adding neutral grape spirits to a base wine once its fermentation stops, then blending meticulously for several years in a complicated cask system known as a *solera*. There are many different styles of sherry, so try them all to see which you prefer: Fino and Manzanilla are delicate, dry, and crisp; Amontillado has a nuttier taste; Oloroso is rich and full flavored, and is made in sweet and dry styles. There is also the incredibly rich sherry known simply as PX (for Pedro Ximénez, the grape it comes from), which is often so luscious that the Spanish pour it over ice cream!

Madeira

If you're getting more adventurous with your choice of aperitifs, here's another one that will pleasure your palate. Madeira (originating from the Portuguese island of the same name) is a fortified wine made in a number of styles, ranging from Malmsey, which is sweet and rich in flavor, to Sercial, which is dry and tangy. Madeiras have a distinctive flavor and aroma and, like ports (see overleaf) they have a long shelf life. The wine has been made since the eighteenth century, and is unusual in that is often placed to age in warm rooms (or attic rafters), where temperatures can reach up to 105°F (40°C), in order to achieve its special "cooked" flavor. Serve it as an aperitif or, if you're a keen chef, try using it in cooking, especially if you want to give a deep, luscious flavor to sauces and gravies.

Port

The very mention of this luscious beverage inspires thoughts of civilised relaxation. When you're in the mood for a sweet, rich, strong wine after dinner that will go well with a cigar or with chocolates, port is just perfect. It's a "fortified" wine, which means grape spirits are added to a base wine during fermentation. Port originated in Portugal (hence the name), but port-style wines are now made around the world. Ruby and tawny ports are aged in wood barrels, and vintage port is sometimes aged in the bottle for ten to forty years. The taste varies from robustly fruity to subtle, dry, and nutty.

Dessert wines

Sweet and chic? But of course! A beautifully made dessert wine is a masterpiece of the winemaker's art. And by choosing a really good dessert wine, you'll be displaying your own good taste. Next time you're in a wine store, spend some time looking at the dessert wines on offer. Some are the result of a special process called "noble rot" or botrytis: a fungus that infects grapes and concentrates their sweetness. They are often called "late-harvest wines" in the United States, while in other countries, particularly Germany and France, "late-harvest" wines are made with or without botrytized grapes. Dessert wines are usually made from Riesling, Sauvignon Blanc, Sémillon, and Gewürztraminer grape varieties. They taste rich and honeyed and have dense textures. Other sweet wines drunk at the end of a meal, such as those made from the Moscato grape, are picked at a normal ripeness with normal sugar levels, but fermentation is stopped before all the sugar has been converted to alcohol, resulting in a sweeter wine. Sometimes, this kind of wine can also have a bit of a fizz on the tongue.

Ice wine

If you want a show-stopping dessert wine, choose an ice wine (Eiswein in Germany, where it originated). It is deep and rich in color, aroma, and flavor. Riesling grapes are commonly used to make ice wines, which are served cold—but do hold the ice! Originally from Germany and Austria, ice wine is also made in Canada and a few other cold regions. Grapes for this dessert wine are picked in the dead of winter while the grapes are frozen on the vines. When they are pressed, most of the water content of the berries is left behind in the form of ice crystals and the remaining juice is highly concentrated and intensely aromatic. Because of the extra care taken to produce ice wines and the fact that making it is a risky proposition, they tend to be high-priced.

when you're

out and about

Ordering wine when you're socializing with other people can be unnerving. You don't want to look like a complete wine illiterate, and at the same time, you want to enjoy a really nice bottle. So how can you tell which is the perfect wine for you from all those choices on the wine list? And what do the names mean, anyway? Don't panic! There are ways to ensure that you get something that will be just to your taste. First, check if the restaurant has a *sommelier* (a specialist wine waiter). If it does, you're in luck. He or she will have in-depth knowledge of the wines on offer. Calling upon that expertise makes great sense—but to get the most from your *sommelier*, it's useful to have an overall idea of what to expect from a wide range of wines. Then you can express your preferences with greater confidence and clarity. And if you're not happy with your wine, it's essential to know whether you have a good reason for sending the bottle back.

Ordering restaurant wines

Ask questions. That's what *sommeliers* and even regular waiters are there for. You don't need to know wine names or how to pronounce long foreign words; simply describe what you like (red, white, sparkling, or rosé; light, sheer flavors or deep, bold ones) and ask to be steered in the right direction. Then, ask for taste samples. Can't decide between the rosé and the Muscadet? Never had a Syrah/Pinot Noir blend before? Ask to try all three. In both restaurants and retail stores, it is often possible to get small tastes of wine, and this is by far the best way to "preview" a wine. After all, someone else's "sheer and light" might taste "bold and deep" to you.

Keep experimenting

The more new wines you try, the more accurately informed your choices will become. You'll develop your own preferences, and feel more confident each time the wine list comes around. If you and your friends always have Chardonnay with your Saturday lunch, try something new next time. If what you usually drink is a California Chardonnay, try one from Australia. Or go further: order a Sauvignon Blanc or a Pinot Grigio. If no one at the table has ever tasted it before and you're reluctant to order a bottle, it's perfectly okay to ask for a taste, a glass or a half-bottle to preview it.

Ordering for the table

If your companions are shy about it, order for the table. Ask your friends or business associates if they usually drink red or white wines: often, there will be mixed preferences. If so, a light-bodied red, such as Pinot Noir, or a heavier white, such as Viognier or an oaky Chardonnay, will do the trick. Half-bottles or half-carafes of several wines are also a good idea. Calculate about a half-bottle per person if your companions are wine-lovers and are drinking moderately, less if it's midday or if other activities are on the agenda after the meal.

The ABC of reading a wine list

A wine list can be presented in various ways, often depending upon the way the *sommelier* has organized it. For instance, it can be divided very simply into red and white wines, or can be listed according to the grape variety used (such as Merlot or Chardonnay), by the wine regions where the wine originates (such as Burgundy or Oregon), or by price. A good wine list will offer wines in several price tiers, so you can indicate to the waiter or *sommelier* how much you'd like to spend. Good wine lists include well-known producers and wine regions so diners can recognize wine they have drunk and enjoyed—or not enjoyed—in the past. But there are better, even more exciting wine lists: these also include some maverick wine producers, emerging wine areas, or new grape varieties, so every diner can be pleased, from the tradition-bound to the more adventurous.

A progressive wine list

This type of wine list divides wines into categories according to flavor profiles. There may be a category for "Light, Dry White Wines" and another for "Medium to Full-bodied Oak-aged White Wines." Each category of red, white, and sparkling wine begins with lighter wines and progresses to heavier ones. This type of wine list is meant to help people who are not sure of their personal preferences or are unsure which wines might match their taste. It can also be helpful in ordering food to accompany wine because, generally, a "Light, Dry White" best matches light cuisine and a "Full-bodied Red" wine suits heartier fare. (See Chapter 8, pages 104–15 for more information on pairing food with wine.)

Flights of wine

Some restaurants or bars in large cities or wine-country regions have flights of wine listed on their menus. A flight is a coordinated series of three or more different, but related, wines served side by side in smaller amounts than a usual glass, but larger than a simple taste. There may be a flight of rosés, two from different regions of France and one from California. Or the flight might be three Tempranillos, all from Spain and from the same vintage, but from three different Spanish wineries. Another popular idea is the same Burgundy from the same producer, but three different years (or vintages). Actually, I think this is a great route toward becoming a wine expert—the best way to learn about wines is to taste them side by side. Flights are not only great fun to sample, they are also a great source of wine education.

Checking the bottle

The person who orders the wine for the table (in this case, you) is usually presented with the bottle. Sometimes there is a little fanfare in the gesture. This may seem intimidating, but calls for nothing more than reading the label to make sure that it is the wine that you ordered. Check not only the name of the winery and wine type (Chardonnay, Pinot Gris, etc.) but also the vintage, or year, that you ordered from the list. It may seem like a small detail, but in some wine-growing regions with variable weather—Oregon, for instance—the vintage can make a really big difference to the quality of a wine. How do you know one vintage from another? You don't. That's what your server or *sommelier* is there for.

Your first taste

The server should always open the bottle at the table—not bring out an open bottle. When the cork is pulled out, it may be handed to you so you can make sure it bears the markings of the wine producer detailed on the label. There's no need to smell the cork: You can tell much more about a wine from its aroma in the glass. Your server should pour a small amount of wine for you to smell and taste. If all eyes are on you, simply act like a pro. Hold the glass by the stem, swirl the wine around in the glass a few times to release the aromas, bring the glass to your nose, and sniff. Then taste. When you taste, swish the wine around a little in your mouth. In most cases, the wine will be fine. Indicate this to the server so he or she can pour for the table.

New glasses?

If you are drinking several wines with your dinner, such as a white with your first course of oysters and a red with your main course of baked salmon, do you ask for new wine glasses when the wine is changed? Yes, but you shouldn't have to. A good server will bring fresh glasses with every change of wine. If you order a second or third bottle of the same wine for the table, that's different. If the wine stays the same, the glasses will, too. Feel free, however, to ask for a new glass if the one you have been using has become smudged by your hands or smells "off."

Returning a bottle

We've all had to face the challenge of sending a wine back, and the experience can be quite nerve-wracking for some people. You shouldn't be scared to return a bottle, but remember, there are particular rules about this. A wine may be "corked," oxidized, or bad because it has been kept in poor storage conditions. That is when you send it back—

not because you've changed your mind and now want a red instead of a white, or because you simply don't like the taste. How to tell whether a wine has turned bad? If a white wine looks honey-colored or a red wine is brownish, they may have oxidized and are no longer good. If there is a musty, wet cardboard smell to the wine, it has been tainted by a bad cork with mold growing in it. If a wine has been improperly stored in temperatures that are either too cold or too hot, or a bottle has been open for several days before you ordered it by the glass, it will taste "off," and you have a right to send it back.

When it's not what you asked for

There is one instance in which you are justified in rejecting a bottle of wine even when you don't think it is flawed. That is when you have conferred with a *sommelier* before ordering and he or she recommends and brings you a wine that you told her you would not like. For example, if you clearly stated that you would not like a buttery, heavily oaked Chardonnay and you are brought a bottle that is oily, rich and oak-tasting, tell the wine steward it is exactly what you said you did not like, and ask him/her to find something else. If it is the opposite of what you discussed in advance, feel comfortable saying so.

How much to pay in a restaurant

Everybody's got to make a living, and most restaurants make theirs by doubling or even tripling the wholesale price they pay for wines they serve you. A ten dollar wine at wholesale becomes a twenty to thirty dollar wine on a restaurant wine list—sometimes more. Restaurants make even more money selling wine by the glass. Destination restaurants sometimes charge for a glass what they paid for the whole bottle (a bottle holds about four and a half glasses). Many wine consumers object to this and even boycott restaurants that mark up the price of a wine too much. Restaurants defend the practice by saying they make most of their profits on wine and other alcoholic drinks because food preparation is so labor-intensive.

Don't be afraid to be cheap!

At least once in your life (maybe more often) order the cheapest bottle of wine on the menu. Often, especially in a "good" restaurant, you will get a treat—a delicious wine at a value price. Wine buyers at restaurants often report that they seldom have a hard time unloading the most expensive wines on their lists, but have more difficulty selling at the other end of the scale. And, they say, no wine would make their list if it wasn't good!

What is a corkage fee?

"Corkage" or a "corkage fee" is what a restaurant charges to open and serve a bottle of wine that you bring into the restaurant. In some places, laws may forbid this practice, but where it is allowed, some restaurants charge no corkage fee, some charge most customers but not local residents, and some charge outrageous fees all the time to anyone! Be sure to call ahead and ask what a restaurant's policy is before you bring along a special bottle. You should not bring a bottle on the restaurant's wine list. Most restaurants uphold a corkage-fee policy to discourage diners from bringing their own wine.

Can you take leftover wine home?

It is not common practice, but some people like to take unfinished wine home, especially when there is a considerable amount left in the bottle. This is not always legal, so it is best to check with your server or *sommelier*.

What to expect from a wine

Wine experts say wines are good when they are "ripe," "balanced," and "well-focused," with "long, lingering aftertastes." They are bad when they lack these essentials and when their "tannins," "acidity" or "oak flavors" dominate the wine. But what do these words mean? If they mean nothing to you, throw them out! What counts most is your own pleasure, and just as a fingerprint is unique, so is every set of taste buds. You may enjoy a wine your spouse finds too sweet, too strong, or boring. But just as you don't feel embarrassed or "uneducated" because you don't like Gorgonzola cheese or lamb, you should not feel deficient if you don't also like the dense, chewy Zinfandel or crisp Sauvignon Blanc your friends are raving about. Having said that, it's really useful to know what to expect from certain wines. Here's the lowdown:

Barbera

Sometimes called "the people's wine" of Piedmont, this wine competes with Sangiovese as Italy's most common and popular red wine. The wine will usually be crisp and easy to drink, not dense and chewy. A Barbera should have a deep ruby color, berry flavors, a medium body, refreshing acidity, and low tannin levels (tannins are those things that make your mouth pucker). Drink it with or without food, and take it along or order it anywhere from a formal dinner party to a summer picnic.

Bordeaux

This wine is what has given the preeminent red-wine region in the world, the Bordeaux area of France, its classy reputation. These are dense red wines that are usually a blend of Cabernet Sauvignon, Cabernet Franc, and Merlot. They are known for their finesse and high quality, and are among the most expensive wines in the world. They are perhaps most valued for their longevity, so if you see such a wine and it is older than anything else on the wine list, don't be put off. Bordeaux is also sometimes called "claret."

Cabernet Franc

Native to Bordeaux, this dry red wine is often a part of a Bordeaux blend (along with Cabernet Sauvignon and Merlot), but can also stand alone. A fleshy, full-flavored, 100 percent Cabernet Franc can simply be too powerful for some people. The wine boasts a blood-red color with possible aromas of pine needles, dried grass, and crushed violets. Expect a velvety texture and flavors of burnt caramel, cherry, or cranberry. Drink this wine with hearty grilled meats and vegetables. As the basis for a dry rosé, Cabernet Franc can provide fresh strawberry flavors.

Cabernet Sauvignon

A true classic, and popular world-wide, this dry red wine comes from the king of French wine grapes, the Cabernet Sauvignon. The character of a particular bottle can range from opulent, as in many Napa Valley versions, to elegant and smooth, as in French examples. Good Cabernets are also produced in Chile, Australia, and Argentina. Most of them are finely made and highly priced, but there is certainly no shortage—that's because Cabernet Sauvignon is among the most widely planted wine-grape varieties in the world. You can expect intense, dark-fruit flavors (such as black cherry, blackberry, and cassis) and fruity aromas. This is a wine that ages very well; it should not be drunk too young. Drink it alone or with grilled red meats, sausages, or strong cheeses. Many wineries make wines that are 100 percent Cabernet, others blend in small amounts of Merlot or Cabernet Franc.

Carmenère

A deeply colored, full-bodied, dry, and sometimes powerful red wine that comes mainly from Chile, where until recently it was often confused with Merlot in the vineyards. It is sometimes blended with Cabernet Sauvignon or stands on its own. The grape, originally used in France, is becoming the emblematic grape of Chile, where the climate and soils of its northern wine-producing valleys offer ideal growing conditions. Expect aromas of spice, jam, raspberry, and dark chocolate, and flavors of tobacco, fig, and chocolate. Drink with hearty dishes containing red meat or beans, robust pasta sauces, and grilled red meats.

Champagne

The famous sparkling wine that originates from the Champagne region of France will almost always be a blend of Chardonnay, Pinot Noir, and Pinot Meunier grapes. In deference to the area where the original champagne method (*méthode champenoise*) was invented, most producers outside Champagne who make the same beverage call theirs "sparkling wine." Under French law, winemakers outside the Champagne region are prohibited from using the word "Champagne" on their labels, but few non-European producers feel bound by this. You should not assume that sparkling wines are inherently inferior to Champagne—they're not—they merely come from another region. You should expect a pale-straw color (pale-salmon for a rosé Champagne) and flavors of strawberry, redcurrant, nutmeg, spice, peach, blackberry, apple or pear. Many Champagnes are dry (brut), delicate, and crisp, but some are creamier and sweeter. Don't save Champagne or sparkling wine for caviar or wedding cake; drink it with mussels, oysters, wild mushrooms, roasted chicken, and roast pork tenderloin.

Chardonnay

This grape hails from the Burgundy region of France and is wildly popular in the United States. Because it grows well in a variety of climates and sites, there are good Chardonnays from almost all wine regions of the world, especially (if you prefer the full-bodied type) California and Australia. The aroma of the wine can sometimes be buttery. The flavor varies according to where it's grown and the style of the winemaker—it can range from clean, crisp, and minerally (as in fine Chablis) to fruity, rich, and toasty if it has been aged in oak barrels. From most Chardonnays, expect flavors of apple, mango, pear, pineapple, lemon, fig, peach, and honey. Drink it on its own, or with grilled chicken, salmon, shrimp, crab, lobster, light pasta, and lightly spiced foods.

Chenin Blanc

Mostly from the Loire in France, California, or South Africa, this is usually a soft, off-dry (slightly sweet) white wine made from the Chenin Blanc grape. If French, the bottle could say Vouvray, Montlouis, or Savennières—the specific wine regions the wine comes from. A Chenin Blanc can also be a very sweet dessert wine, as it is a grape that can be raised in several different styles, so be sure to ask before ordering. In a dinner wine, expect a pleasantly fruity, clean taste with flavors of lemon, melon, apple, peach, citrus fruit or camomile that suit the spiciest of ethnic foods.

Gewürztraminer

The German word *Gewürz* means "spice," and is suggestive of the flowery, spicy aromas and flavors of this wine. It can be made in a range of styles from sweet to dry, so make sure the description indicates this. Good Gewürztraminer comes from France, Germany, California, Chile, and other regions. Expect aromas of cinnamon, clove, citrus, peach or apricot. The wine is often recommended as a companion to spicy meals, such as Thai and Indian.

Grenache

Widespread in the Rhône region of France, this fruity red is gaining popularity in the U.S. and Australia. In Spain it is called Garnacha, and in Rioja, it is second in importance to the famous Tempranillo grape. It is often blended with other red grapes, such as Syrah and Cabernet Sauvignon. If the wine is French, some of the best examples will be from Châteauneuf-du-Pape or Gigondas. You can expect full, concentrated wines with aromas of minerals, wet earth, and plums, and flavors that hint of leather, prunes, and roasted chestnuts. Drink this wine with hearty foods, including red meats and strong cheeses.

Malbec

A dry red wine originally used as a blending grape in Bordeaux. Today it is the star grape of Argentina's emerging wine industry and is often grown in the country's high-altitude vineyards. There are also Malbecs or Malbec blends from neighboring Chile. Expect juicy, deep, fruit flavors, such as raspberry, with hints of coffee and cinnamon, along with a lot of tannin. This can be a chewy wine. Drink with grilled red meats, chicken, blood sausages, and even goat (often cooked in a typical Argentine barbecue). Argentine wines are still a relative bargain around the world.

Merlot

This soft, fruity red wine is popular with consumers as an approachable alternative to Cabernet Sauvignon. Grown and made throughout the world, it is widely used in

Bordeaux, France. Expect smooth, fruit flavors of red and black cherry, berry, plum, and redcurrant, with hints of spice, tobacco, and licorice. The aromas and flavors of Merlot can vary widely from vineyard to vineyard and bottle to bottle, so don't expect one to taste exactly like the last Merlot you had. Drink with grilled red meats, hamburgers, tuna and swordfish, pizzas, and stews. Merlot is often consumed younger than most Cabernets.

Muscadet

This dry, clean-tasting white wine comes from the Loire region of France. You can expect a sheer white wine with crisp, light flavors of lemon, apple, pear, grapefruit, minerals, and herbs. Ideally drunk with oysters and other light seafood dishes.

Nebbiolo

This dry red wine is usually a powerhouse of flavor. In Italy, premium wines made from the Nebbiolo grape are considered on a par with the finest French Burgundies. It's the leading grape from Piedmont, Italy, and goes into two of its best known products, Barolo and Barbaresco. When grown in California, where it does well in the cooler, northern part of the state, the label will usually state Nebbiolo on it. Expect flavors of cherry, rose, tobacco, tar, cinnamon, and chocolate truffles. Drink with hearty, stick-to-your-ribs dishes, and grilled meats.

Pinot Grigio

A popular dry white wine made chiefly in Italy, France, Germany, Austria, and Oregon (where it is called Pinot Gris), Pinot Grigio is the top imported wine in the U.S. and its popularity is already beginning to rival that of Chardonnay. Expect rich, spicy, tropical-fruit aromas and flavors in a Pinot Gris from France and a delicate, light, crisp wine with citrus-fruit flavors from Italian versions. Pinot Grigio is usually a modestly priced wine. Drink with lighter cuisine, such as seafood and delicately sauced vegetable or chicken dishes.

Pinot Noir

The fragile, finicky Pinot Noir grape is temperamental—on the one hand it can produce some of the world's most collectible wines, on the other, a thin "breakfast wine" without much life to it. Look for higher-priced Pinot Noirs from Burgundy, Oregon, or the Russian River Valley of California. Expect sumptuous velvety textures, and flavors and aromas of red cherry, raspberry, raisin, violet, and earth. Drink it young, or at five to ten years old at the very most. Pinot Noir is a food-friendly wine to quaff with roasted chicken, duck, pork, salmon, and mushrooms.

Riesling

Consumers still have some misconceptions about Rieslings because they assume they are all sweet wines that don't go with food. But the best Rieslings are dry wines, such as the steely, aromatic Riesling Kabinetts from Germany. Increasingly, Riesling is being grown in many other parts of the world. Styles range from dry to semi-sweet and super-sweet dessert wines. Expect delicate floral aromas, such as jasmine, rose, or orange blossom, and flavors of peach, honeysuckle, nectarine, tangerine, and minerals. Drink with spicy foods, shellfish, chicken, veal, pork, and salads.

Sangiovese

The star grape of Tuscany, perhaps the most idyllic wine region of Italy, Sangiovese produces a dry red wine. Some Sangiovese also comes from California, made by Italian immigrants who want to revive a wine tradition from their homeland. This is the grape that plays a large role in Chianti, the wine in the basket-wrapped bottle. Newer versions from both Tuscany and California now have world-class status. Expect a deep-colored wine that is lighter in texture and flavor than a Cabernet Sauvignon with flavors of red fruit. Sangiovese can also be blended with Cabernet Sauvignon or Merlot in a "Super-Tuscan" wine (see page 125). Drink with pizza, strongly flavored pasta dishes, grilled meats, and sauced vegetable dishes.

Sauvignon Blanc (also called Fumé Blanc)
Originally from France, this is a crisp, dry white wine that is now made in many countries. New Zealand is the main player in the New World, while Chile is also producing impressive examples. Expect aromas and flavors of lemon, pear, melon, apple, grapefruit, hay, or grass. Drink it with light cuisine, such as shellfish, sole and halibut, chicken, salads, vegetables, and citrus-fruit sauces. Sauvignon Blanc can also be a very sweet dessert wine similar to Sauternes.

Syrah (also called Shiraz in Australia)
Syrah originates in the Rhône region of France, but is also grown in many parts of the United States and has become one of Australia's star wines. Expect a spicy, full-flavored wine with aromas and flavors of blackberry, cherry, sage, and leather. Don't drink it too young: It needs time to age and smooth out. Drink with grilled red meats, wild game, and stews. There is no relation between Syrah and the wine known as Petite Sirah.

Tempranillo
King of Spanish wines, this dry red often stands alone, but can also be blended with other grapes, such as Grenache. It

is an elegant wine, with concentrated, dark-fruit flavors, that ages very well. In fact, some are made not to drink young, so don't be afraid to order those that have been in the bottle for several years. Expect aromas of fruit jam and hints of smoke, pepper, and other spices, like clove and cinnamon. Drink with grilled meats, strong cheese, and strongly flavored vegetable dishes with spicy sauces.

Zinfandel

Often called the most American of wine grapes and a popular favorite at the Thanksgiving holiday meal, Zinfandel is chiefly cultivated in California. Though it was once thought to have descended from Italy's Primitivo grape, recent research at the University of California, Davis, has traced its roots back to Croatia. Expect a bold red wine with aromas of black pepper and flavors of cranberry, plum, raisin, raspberry, red cherry, and boysenberry. Don't drink it too young, as this wine needs aging to settle its acidity. Drink Zinfandel with sausages, ribs and beef, tomato sauces, pizza, Cajun dishes, and grilled vegetables.

Viognier

This is a great Chardonnay alternative. Originally from the Rhône area of France and made also in various parts of California, Viognier is a stylish, full-bodied, dry white wine with a touch of the spiciness of a Gewürztraminer. Expect flavors of honeysuckle, peach, citrus fruit, minerals, and apricot. Drink it to accompany light snacks, such as olives or raw vegetables, or with light cuisine, including seafood, chicken, and pork with light sauces.

White Zinfandel

Called a "blush" wine because of its pretty pink color, this fruity wine was invented in the Napa Valley in the 1970s and became so popular it is often credited with boosting wine consumption in the U.S. It is a soft white wine made from the hearty red Zinfandel grape. The blush color is achieved by removing the red skins from the grape pulp and juice within a few hours of crushing so that the juice's tint is light rather than a deep red color. Expect a somewhat sweet wine, with aromas of strawberry and watermelon, that goes down easily and complements many foods, especially those with some heat, such as Asian or Latin cuisine.

Say it with confidence

One of the most often-cited reasons for the lack of popularity of some wines, especially German, French, and Italian, is that people are intimidated to order them because they don't know how to pronounce the names! Here are some tongue twisters that you should not hesitate to try:

Gewürztraminer (German)—Ga-VURTZ-tra-mee-ner

Viognier (French)—VEE-oh-nyay

Sauvignon Blanc (French)—Sow-vee-nyawn-BLAWNK

Pinot Noir (French)—PEE-no Nwhar

Muscadet (French)—Mus-ka-DAY

Pinot Grigio (Italian)—PEE-no GREE-joe

Sangiovese (Italian)—San-joe-VAY-zee

Nebbiolo (Italian)—Neb-ee-OH-lo

Tempranillo (Spanish)—Tem-pra-NEE-yo

Claret (British English)—cla-ret: Pronounce the "a" like the "a" in "cat," and the "et" as in "forget."

how to

3

buy wine

When you know what you like to drink, buying wine can be utterly pleasurable. But if you're not wine savvy, and don't know one bottle from another, it can be a tense nightmare. Decisions, decisions. How to select from all those names and places? Faced with an array of bottles, it's tempting to pick up the nearest one, hand over your money, and get out of there fast. But that way you'd be missing so much. You need a strategy! The best is to be utterly shameless: Confess to everyone—friends, wine waiters, clerks at wine stores—that you would like help and advice with buying wine. You'll be amazed at how willing people are to impart their knowledge. The owner of your small, local wine shop will have more time to talk to you and get to know your likes and dislikes than clerks at larger stores. As for worrying about how much to spend, set a realistic amount that you can afford, then relax. You'll discover excellent, drinkable wines in all price ranges.

How to get help in the store

Don't be shy! Ask for a knowledgeable salesperson, or shop only at stores with staff trained to help customers make decisions. Most quality wine shops offer this service, and a growing number of supermarkets and upscale groceries do also. These people are familiar with the wines they sell and can steer you in the right direction once they know your preferences, your budget, and the occasion you're buying for, whether it's a special anniversary or a rainy-night dinner at home.

What's your "style?"

Just as different people have personal styles, so does wine. When you walk into a retail store and ask a salesperson for help, one of the first questions you're likely to be asked is what type of wine you like. Good question! But it is not enough to say "white," or even "Chardonnay." Many French Chardonnays can be crisp and lean; those from California can be buttery and oak-tasting; and in yet another style, those from Australia can be oily, fruity powerhouses of flavor. If you're smitten with one of these styles, it would be a disappointment to get one of the others. So think about wine style as a starting point to buying wines that you will personally enjoy.

Taste it first

Many fine-wine shops offer wine tasting, so you can sample before buying. There is no better way to tell if you will enjoy a new wine. Some stores schedule wine tastings for a certain day at a certain time, so ask about your shop's program. Talk to the salespeople who are pouring. Ask what they taste in the wine you are trying and see if you also taste the cassis or black pepper that they noted. You're not wrong if you don't; trying wines this way is simply part of your education. In these free tastings, sample new wines that you might hesitate to order in a restaurant.

Where to shop

Fine-wine shop in the best part of town? Discount beverage warehouse on the wrong side of the tracks? Where is the best place to buy your wine? Look for a store that is service-oriented, one that tries to determine its customers' preferences over a period of time by finding out the types of foods they enjoy, the grape varieties they prefer, and the people they socialize with. This may mean a small shop in your area, but it may mean a larger store, too. Look for those that have been around a long time; this indicates they're good at what they do. When you develop a relationship with a favorite retailer, let them understand you and your tastes better by giving them feedback after you drink the wines they have sold you.

Quality control

Make sure you buy wine on a regular basis from stores that take proper care of their inventory. Direct sunlight, extreme heat or cold, and dramatic temperature fluctuations can ruin wine before it is even opened. If you notice any of these conditions when you're inside the store, look for another place to purchase your wine. To check a specific bottle while you are in the store, make sure that the liquid in the bottle reaches its neck, that the cork is not pushing out of the bottle, and that there are no signs of leakage.

Wine clubs

In this age of high technology, you can shop for wine with your computer or by telephone. Wine clubs, prevalent in the U.S. and Australia, are increasing in popularity everywhere, and are a convenient way to shop for yourself or give gifts to the wine-lovers in your life. Wine clubs are usually sponsored by wineries, which sell only their own wines, plus gifts and memorabilia from their winery retail stores. Wine-club memberships can vary from one to twelve months, and depending on the winery, also can vary quite a bit in price, but all wines are discounted to members. Shipping within the U.S. can be tricky because of interstate shipping laws involving alcohol, so make sure you visit the web site (or call the toll-free number) of the winery you are interested in to determine if they can ship to you. Most U.S. wineries can ship to at least a dozen states, some many more. Clubs may also be separate commercial enterprises not affiliated to any one winery. A caveat: Some wine retailers say wine clubs are often clearing houses for well-known producers to sell off inferior vintages quickly.

Retail prices

Traditional mark-ups on wines for retail stores, such as your corner fine-wine shop, are 50 percent over the wholesale price the store pays to a distributor. So a bottle that costs the retail shop ten dollars will be marked up to fifteen on the retail shelf. There are exceptions; some retailers offer discounts because they get discounts on volume purchases, so watch for bins full of specials. But with so many good wines being made and exported from Europe, California, Chile, Argentina, South Africa, New Zealand, and Australia, you need not spend a lot of money to get your wine education going or even to deepen it.

Should I buy at the winery?

In terms of price, the winery is often the worst place to shop because most wineries do not have sales. They offer their wines at suggested retail prices because they know most people visiting the winery are on vacation and in the mood to spend money! That's why so many retail shops at wineries these days contain not only the wines they produce but gifts, food, wine paraphernalia, and even clothes. But many wineries make small-production wines that never go into retail stores and are available only at the winery. If you taste such a wine and like it, you may well wish to buy some, even if it's not bargained-priced.

Cheaper by the dozen

Most retail stores offer discounts of 10–15 percent on purchases of twelve or more bottles, so when you discover a wine you especially like, consider buying it by the case, which is usually twelve bottles (for extremely limited-production wines, a case may comprise six bottles). High-quality wines of limited production can be purchased based on the vintage. Wines of "good" quality made in quantities larger than two to three thousand cases are often blended and bottled as needed. So if you find a particularly good 2002 Sauvignon Blanc from a California winery and wish to purchase a case of it, ask your salesperson to check the lot number or bottling date on the box. By doing so you can be reasonably sure that the glass you enjoyed last night will be the same wine you buy today.

Why vintage matters

Vintage, the year the grapes were harvested and the wines made, is extremely important in some wine-growing areas of the world, less so in others. The most important element of a good vintage is the quality of the grapes. Most wineries would sacrifice an abundant harvest for excellent quality grapes any year. A good "year," or vintage, means that the right weather conditions have produced the best grapes. With modern farming methods and winemaking techniques, some areas with consistent, reliable weather, such as California's Napa Valley, view bad harvests as a thing of the past. That does not mean there won't be differences in each vintage, but there will be very few vintages that bomb completely. In other areas, such as Bordeaux or rainy Oregon, the weather is more variable and unpredictable. So, too, is the quality of the wine produced from year to year.

Bottle shapes

Bottle shapes vary widely and their individual styles are mostly founded on the local traditions of a region or industry. Probably the single most important factor in a bottle's shape is that it lends itself to being laid on its side for storage in order to keep the cork moist. Some producers will not put their wines in clear glass because they believe that exposure to light could harm the wine, but others prefer clear glass to display the wine's color. Look for browning in older whites and rosés when bottled in clear glass. It is a good indication that the wine is on the downhill side of drinkability.

Sizing up bottles

The standard wine bottle size is 750 milliliters, which yields about four and a half glasses of wine. Gaining in popularity are 375 milliliter bottles, also called half bottles, because of the flexibility they offer consumers. Other bottle sizes you may encounter include "splits," used only for Champagne, that hold 187 milliliters of wine (one serving) and large-format bottles, such as magnums that hold one and a half liters or two standard bottles of wine, jeroboams (also called three-liter bottles), and double magnums. Don't ever try to pour the largest sized bottle of wine, the Nebuchadnezzar, by yourself—it holds fifteen liters, or twenty standard bottles.

The dent in the bottom

There's a special word for that dent on the bottom of a wine bottle—it's called a "punt." It is found on the bottom of Champagne/sparkling-wine bottles and some still wine bottles. The main purpose of the rounded bottom, or punt, is to strengthen the bottle—especially important for sparkling wines—but punts also can be useful for collecting sediment. You might find the punt helpful when pouring wine, since it provides a secure place to put your thumb.

Can I return a bottle of wine to a store?

Yes, but only when there is something wrong with it. The wine could be "corked," meaning that mold growing in the cork has imparted a moldy taste to the wine, or it could be "oxidized," meaning air has gotten by the cork, turned the wine brownish, and given it a cooked or baked flavor like sherry. Wine-industry insiders say as many as five to ten percent of bottles may be corked. But simply not liking the wine in the bottle is not enough reason to return it.

Relying on names and reputation

Do wine knowledge and tasting ability sometimes seem like competitive sports? Well that's because they are. Wine competitions are passionately contested arenas in which vintners try to distinguish themselves in a highly competitive market. So, winners are impressive. But when you are shopping for wine, should you always stop at the bin that says "Gold Medal Winner?" For some people, using medal winners as consumer aids amounts to a safe bet that discourages them from learning their own tastes. For others, especially those uncomfortable with wine, having a gold medal attached to a wine is definitely a recommendation of quality and will encourage them to try something they might not otherwise.

Do wine writers help?

Well, I'm always delighted when someone says they like my recommendations! In fact the best strategy is to calibrate your tastes with a writer's. You'll discover some writers who give high marks to wines that are robust, tannic, and filled with character even if the wines may be flawed. The reasoning is that, if a winemaker is willing to walk that tightrope of making "imperfect" wines to offer the consumer a beverage that is full of personality, then "bravo!" Another writer might be more inclined to give higher scores to wines that technically strive for perfection, even if this limits the audience to the fringes of the consumer spectrum. A wine writer may declare he hardly ever drinks white wine, and prefers strong reds. If you prefer white wines, this is hardly helpful, so try to find a critic who seems open-minded and reflects your tastes as closely as possible.

What to look for in wine labels

Although they vary in some ways from country to country, most wine labels in most languages contain the following information: the name of the wine, the vintage year, the estate, château, winery or producer that made the wine, a quality designation, the alcohol content, the volume of wine in the bottle, the country of origin, and the more specific appellation, or geographic area, from which the wine hails. A label might also say what specific grape varieties were used for the wine, and whether it is red, white, rosé, or sparkling.

Should I judge a wine by its label?

No, except when labels are so whimsical or fun that you want the bottle just for the label. Fancy labels and fine packaging are sometimes designed to send a message to the consumer: "I look expensive, I am expensive, I am worth it!" In medium-priced categories where competition among wines is fiercest, wine producers know that eye-catching, colorful labels are important to attract consumers' attention when their product is on the shelf with hundreds of others. Wines with long, established histories have built their brands over many years and rely on elegant, understated packaging that remains unchanged from vintage to vintage.

Every label tells a story

So, you're in the store surrounded by a dizzying array of bottles. As you browse, you'll probably zero in on a few labels. Wine labels can generally be divided into two types: those that highlight the grape variety used (Merlot, for example) and others that mention the geographic area in which the wine grapes were grown and/or in which the wine was made. Wines from the United States, Australia, New Zealand, and South America fall into the "grape variety" category. If they contain the name of a grape variety, they must contain at least seventy-five percent of that grape; the rest can be one or two other grape varieties that the winemaker feels balance out the primary source. On the following pages are some 'virtual' wine labels devised to give you an idea of what to look for.

French wine labels

If you like French wine and plan to buy lots of it, you will want to know a little about how to read wine labels in France. The wine label generally highlights the sub-region from which the wine comes (such as Pauillac or Margaux, both within the Bordeaux region) over the grape variety (such as Chardonnay or Merlot) because the French traditionally exalt place over everything. In fact, in many cases a wine producer is forbidden from stating the name of the grape variety on the label. So you need to learn the prominent varieties in each region. For example, the Sancerre appellation is known primarily for Sauvignon Blanc. A French label may also list the classification of the château or region. Take the classification *premier cru*, which means "first growth"—this refers to the ranking of the vineyard in which the grapes for that particular wine were grown.

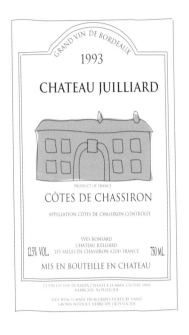

GRAND VIN DE BORDEAUX

1993

CHATEAU JUILLIARD

PRODUCT OF FRANCE

CÔTES DE CHASSIRON

APPELLATION CÔTES DE CHASSIRON CONTRÔLÉE

YVES RONSARD
CHATEAU JUILLIARD
12.5% VOL.   LES SALLES DE CHASSIRON (GDE) FRANCE   750 ML

MIS EN BOUTEILLE EN CHATEAU

CE VIN EST ISSU DE RAISIN CUEILLI À LA MAIN, CULTIVÉ SANS
HERBICIDE, NI PESTICIDE

THIS WINE IS MADE FROM GRAPES PICKED BY HAND,
GROWN WITHOUT HERBICIDE OR PESTICIDE

Italian wine labels

Italian wine labels often detail the name of the grape variety as well as the geographic area in which the wine was made, instead of one or the other. For quality assurance, look for the words *Denominazione di Origine Controllata e*

RAFAELLA

RISERVA

1974

CHIANTI CLASSICO

DENOMINAZIONE DI ORIGINE CONTROLLATA

BOTTLED BY CHIANTI RAFAELLA SNC
FIESOLE ITALIA

750 ML   PRODUCT OF ITALY   ALC 12.5% BY VOL.

Garantita (D.O.C.G.)—this is the highest quality designation in Italy. *Vino da tavola* indicates everyday table wine. Top wine regions, which may be listed on the front label, include Piedmont and Chianti Classico.

German wine labels

Many people say the difficulty of reading German wine labels is one of the chief reasons German wines are not drunk more commonly around the world. But if you like the delicacy and versatility of a German Riesling, or the honeyed richness of an Eiswein, don't let the labels put you off. Perhaps the most important thing to check out on a German label is its quality category. *Qualitätswein mit Prädikat* (shortened to Q.m.P.) is the highest category of German wine quality, so if your bottle says that, you can be reasonably sure you are getting something that is worth trying. *Tafelwein* (table wine) is the lowest quality level of German wine, followed by *Landwein* (which is very similar to French *vin de pays*), but you will probably only encounter these if you are traveling in Germany. Riesling is also the premier grape of Germany, so look out for that— particularly if it is a bottle of Riesling Kabinett.

S.A.Baum

Weingut Nackenheim in Rhein

1985

Nackenheimer Frühling
Riesling Spätlese

Qualitätswein mit Prädikat

GUTTSHABFÜLLUNG

alc. 11.5% vol.   750 ml.

RHEINHESSEN

Another designation that may be found on a German wine label refers to the level of grape ripeness that went into the wine. What does this mean, exactly? The ripeness of the grapes when they are picked to make a wine is crucially important because that level indicates whether a wine will be light in body (and usually dry and lightweight in flavor) or full and rich (and usually sweeter). There is an ascending hierarchy of these ripeness levels, which are determined mainly (though not exclusively) by the sugar content of the grapes before fermentation. *Kabinett* is at the light end of the scale, which moves up to Spätlese, Auslese, Beerenauslese, Rockenbeerenauslese, and Eiswein. The first two are generally dry dinner wines that are reasonably priced, while the last four get noticeably sweeter and more expensive as they move up the scale.

Spanish wine labels

When reading the label of a Spanish wine, look for the chief quality indicator, *Denominación de Origen—Denominación de*

Origen Calificada in the case of Rioja—which indicates that the wine comes from an official wine region and has met certain high standards in the growing of its grapes and the winemaking process. Another quality designation refers to the aging of the wines and the grapes from which they are made. These designations, which are indicated somewhere on the wine label, are *crianza, reserva* or *gran reserva,* the last being the very highest quality level. You should also look on the label for Spain's leading wine regions, such as Rioja, Ribera del Duero, or Priorato.

Australian wine labels

Australia has a long history of winemaking and produces some of the highest quality wines anywhere. Its winemakers are some of the best in the world. Their approach to the rules and laws that govern winemaking is much less tradition-bound than in Europe. So Australian wine labels look much like ones from the United States, and are

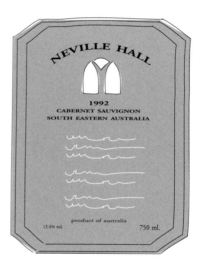

generally clear and unfettered with details. When a grape variety appears on the label, such as Shiraz (the French Syrah), at least 85 percent of that grape must be in the bottle. Otherwise, an Australian wine label will list the winery name, alcohol content, vintage, and wine region.

United States wine labels

America also has a long and proud history of high-quality winemaking. As with Australian wine labels, American labels are refreshingly simple to read and understand. In fact, they are allowed to contain less information than European labels chiefly because there

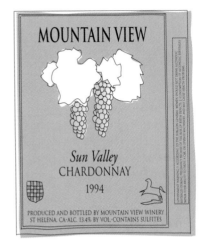

MOUNTAIN VIEW

Sun Valley
CHARDONNAY
1994

PRODUCED AND BOTTLED BY MOUNTAIN VIEW WINERY
ST HELENA, CA·ALC. 13.4% BY VOL.·CONTAINS SULFITES

are fewer regulations and laws governing wine. Usually, the label will contain the name of the winery, the grape variety the wine is primarily made from, the area from which it comes, and the alcohol content. But by federal law, American wine labels must also contain a health warning about the dangers of alcohol consumption that is not found on wines produced in the rest of the world.

What does the term "Vineyard-designated" mean on a bottle of American wine? According to U.S. law, 95 percent of the grapes in a wine must come from one particular vineyard in order for a producer to include the vineyard designation on the label. Wineries include this information to show that the wine in the bottle is not only from a very particular spot, but an esteemed spot that grows the best grapes. You should expect to pay higher prices for wines that mention the specific vineyard from which the grapes originate. Some vineyards are named after the owners' loved ones, and will say something like "Katherine's Vineyard," or "Redhead Vineyard."

You may also find the words "Estate-bottled" on a bottle of American wine. This means that the winery owns and grows the grapes that are in the wine—it's analogous to a restaurant saying its apple pie is "homemade." You may wonder why there is a special term to indicate this; it's because many wineries do not grow their own grapes, but buy them in from grape growers. Some firms don't even make the wine—they buy finished wine from other producers, then sell it under their own labels. Generally speaking, wines that have been grown, nurtured, made, and bottled under one winery's supervision are higher-quality products.

What does "reserve" mean?

In many European wines, this term (*reserve* in French, *riserva*, in Italian, *reserva*, in Spanish) denotes that wines have been aged longer than those not carrying this moniker. But in the United States, there is no legal meaning attached to the word "Reserve" on a wine label. Wineries usually use it to indicate a higher level of quality; and sometimes the term "Reserve" indicates that the wine was made from the finest grapes of the vintage. Expect to pay more for reserve wines.

Appellations

"Appellation of Origin" is a geographic term that indicates where the grapes are grown for a particular wine. There will be some version of this on every bottle of quality wine from almost every country. In Spain, it is indicated by the term *Denominación de Origen*, in France, *Appellation Contrôlée* (these designations also include a set of rules about how the wines are to be made). An American Viticultural Area (A.V.A.) refers to a specific area. To include an A.V.A. on a U.S. wine label, 85 percent of the grapes in the wine must come from the indicated A.V.A. Why should you care? Unlike milk or chocolate, wine is very much about place—that terroir word again. The climate, the soil, and other factors specific to a place figure strongly in a wine's quality and character. So it is a service to you, the consumer, to let you know exactly where a wine comes from.

Alcohol content

Wines made around the world vary in their alcohol content, but a rough range is from 7–15 percent for table wines. Some, such as those from Germany and Portugal, are in the low range of 7–9 percent; others (most red and white wines from California) are in the 11–14 percent range. The alcohol percentage must be printed on the label and is most often found on the front of a wine bottle.

What does "Unfiltered" mean?

This is wine that has not been put through a filtering process to clarify it. Some wine producers choose to filter a wine to remove small particles and achieve greater clarity in the wine. When a wine label says "Unfiltered," the producer has deliberately chosen not to filter the wine, and wants consumers to know it. These wineries believe that filtering a wine during production can harm the wine and create a product with less depth and character.

Back labels

The best back labels contain the date the grapes were harvested, the varietal percentage if the wine is a blend of grapes, what type of oak was used in the aging, and the number of months the wine spent in barrels. This is often where you find "chatty" information about the history of the winery, type of wine, and family who made it.

What does "Contains Sulfites" mean?

Many wine labels, such as those from the U.S., say "Contains Sulfites" on the back label. Use of sulfites in wine dates back over two thousand years, but the mandatory inclusion of this information on the label by some countries is recent. Winemakers add a very small amount of sulfites, or sulfur dioxide, to wine to slow oxidation, which, over time, turns wine brown and leads to a cooked flavor and loss of fruitiness. People hypersensitive to sulfites could suffer an asthmatic attack after drinking wine, but, for all but a few, the low level of sulfites in wine presents no health hazard. If you are sensitive to sulfites, you would probably have discovered it before you were old enough to drink wine, since sulfites are often used to preserve the freshness of shrimp and lettuce in salad bars. Very few wines are 100 percent sulfite-free. You may have heard that sulfites in red wines cause headaches and congestion, but this popular belief is mistaken. Indeed, a typical red wine contains fewer sulfites than a typical white wine. More likely to cause such symptoms are histamines in grape skins. Red wine affects a histamine-sensitive drinker more than white since it has spent more time in contact with grape skins.

how to

4

taste wine

Tasting wine with quiet thought, concentration, and deliberation can be a revelation. You become highly aware of how sensitive your taste buds are—and how they combine with your sense of smell to tell you about the wine you are swishing around inside your mouth. Yes, you do need to do that—it's not some silly affectation. In fact, it's a really good way to let your taste buds (and your sense of smell) detect the finer flavors of the wine you are sampling. And what flavors you'll discover! Hints of chocolate, vanilla, herbs, even smoke, evoking all kinds of taste and aroma memories. Wine tasting is not reserved for the experts— anyone can learn how to do it. What's more, it's an experience that's great to share, so why not hold your own wine tasting with friends? You'll find the more you try out different wines, and the more attention you pay to each one, the more expert you'll become at assessing a wine's quality and characteristics.

The basics of wine tasting

There's no need to fuss—tasting wine is not that complicated. You need the wine, of course, a few glasses suited to the type of wine you are drinking (see below), and a corkscrew you are comfortable with (see pages 80–81). Professional tasters are usually provided with a selection of plain nibbles, like crackers or bread, to cleanse the palate between wines. Again, this is not just an affectation but a good idea if you want a pure taste of more than one wine and don't want one to affect another.

Using your nose

It may not be immediately obvious, but your nose, not your tongue, is the best tool for tasting wine. Why? Because your tongue recognizes only a handful of tastes, among them sweet, sour, bitter, and salty. But your nose can identify thousands of substances. The reason you see wine experts make a big show of swirling their glasses, bringing the glass to their noses and inhaling is because smell is so important in taste perception. Most of what we think of as "taste" is actually odor. Just think about how the taste of food changes when you have a bad cold and cannot smell. Smelling wine is not just an affectation, but the best way to tell if it is good or pleasing to you.

Your nose remembers

Aromas can help your brain remember things—like your grandmother's house, the garden in your childhood home, or your favorite leather jacket. The same is true of the wines you've drunk, since wine is something experienced primarily through the sense of smell. When you take the time to smell a wine and record its aromas in your brain, you are helping to store away a piece of knowledge about your personal wine likes and dislikes.

How should wine smell?

The way a wine smells is dependent on many factors, including the variety of the grape, the wine style, and different winemaking techniques. But in general, a wine should smell clean, fresh, and rather like fruit. If it smells like moldy cheese, vinegar or wet cardboard, there is probably something wrong with it. (See below.)

If a wine smells bad

An instinctive feeling of revulsion is usually accurate—the wine probably is bad. Faulty corks cause wine to smell like moldy cheese or wet newspapers (see page 23–24 for "corked" wines). A vinegar smell probably means the wine has been ruined by acetic acid. An odor of nail polish means ethyl acetate has formed in the bottle and indicates a poorly made red wine. A rotten-egg smell or "barnyard" aroma also means things have gone wrong in the wine. Aromas of sour milk are caused by an organism called lactobacillus that spoils wine. None of these poison you, but they all indicate inferior or spoiled wines and if smells are present to the point that you can detect them, they will also produce bitter, sharp, dry, sour, or moldy flavors.

Choosing wine glasses

Although it's true that wine can be drunk from any kind of glass—even a paper cup or a leather bag—the right glass can enhance your experience. When buying wine glasses, there are a few important points to keep in mind. Thin glass is better than thick. A thin, smooth rim beats the extra ridge, or lip, of glass that cheaper wine glasses often have. Clear glass is better than colored so you can see the wine's color. And the size and shape of the bowl of the glass can truly affect the wine's taste. (See pages 84–88 for more information on wine glasses.)

Start with a clean glass

This may seem elementary, but it is important to make sure your wine glasses are meticulously clean and not used for other things, especially milk or ice cream. That's because dairy products can leave residue on the inside of the glass that interferes with the delicate flavors and aromas of the wine and obscures its clarity and color.

How to hold your wine glass

The reason most wine glasses have a stem is because you are supposed to hold them by the stem and not smudge the glass bowl with your fingertips. This allows you to better see the color and clarity of the wine. When your hands touch the bowl of the glass, body heat warms the wine a bit, so if your wine is too cold, there may be a point to holding it the "wrong" way.

How to swirl

Professional wine tasters have oodles of confidence. They can effortlessly swirl the wine in the glass without spilling a drop. Don't try that yourself without plenty of practice. The safest way is to place your glass on a secure table in front of you and hold it by its stem at the lower end, between your thumb and index finger or your first two fingers, whichever feels more comfortable. Rotate the glass in a circular motion fast enough that the wine swirls around in the glass, but not so fast that it spills over. This is why professionals and wine-knowledgeable people never fill a glass to the brim.

Why you swirl

You swirl the wine in your glass to get the most out of a wine's aroma. The motion releases the aromas of the wine so that you are better able to appreciate them. The smell of a wine should be an enticing prelude to what you are about to taste, so don't deny yourself the experience! In a young wine, you should detect fruit and maybe the smell of the barrels it was aged in. If the wine is older, you'll notice less fruit and more complexity.

Take a good sniff

After you've swirled your wine a few times, put your nose into the center of the glass. The aromas are enclosed there, so your nose should not be too distant. Inhale a few times. If you do not get any smell, swirl again, then sniff again. Some wines need to sit in the glass for a while before they "open up" and offer their full-on aromas.

Look at the wine

Use another of your senses—your sight—to take a good look at your wine before you quaff it. The real pro holds the glass against a clean white background for perfect viewing. A winemaker will give a lot of attention to a wine's color and it is usually an eye-pleasing aspect of the drink. Whether it is the deep, ruby color of a Cabernet Sauvignon, the pale-salmon of a rosé, or the honeyed amber of a dessert wine, wine can look arresting as well as appetizing on the dinner table, buffet table, or in your glass.

Red wine color

When you are first served a wine, hold the glass at an angle so the wine is almost sideways in the glass against a light or white background in a well-lit room. Look for clarity and a deep purple or brick red in a red wine. The color comes from the contact of grape juice with grape skins during the winemaking process and, in the making of red wines, this can be an extended period. Older red wines grow less intense in color as they age. Red wines will lose some of their cherry redness or purplish hue and take on a brownish tone. If you see a brownish tint around the edge of the wine in your glass in a young red wine, beware, as it has probably oxidized prematurely and won't be good to drink.

White wine color

Look for clarity and a pale-straw, light-green, or gold color in a white wine. White wines are pale because their juice is pressed immediately and does not come into extended contact with grape skins during the winemaking process. All older white wines deepen in color and grow more golden with age. If a young white has a brownish tinge, there is probably something wrong with it.

Wine sludge

If you notice solids collected at the bottom of your glass or bottle of wine, especially in an older wine, this is not a sign that something is wrong. Older wines sometimes contain "sediment" in the bottle. It is not bad for you and won't affect the taste of the wine, but many people find it unappealing to look at or to feel on the tongue. Decanting, pouring the wine into another container and leaving the sediment behind in the bottle, usually does the trick. (See page 83–84 for how to decant) If you are not entertaining, you may simply want to pour from the bottle through a small, fine-meshed strainer directly into your glass.

Clear your palate first

To effectively taste the wine, you should make sure you do not have a riot of flavors coating your mouth and fighting your taste buds before you try it. Let's say you have never tried a wine before and want to see if you will like the grape variety or the style of a certain wine producer. Make sure your first few sips (and take a few, since your mouth must adapt to the wine) are not clouded by a horseradish-encrusted halibut or a pizza liberally sprinkled with hot red pepper. After you've really tasted the wine, then feel free to go ahead and try drinking it with your hot peppers or horseradish. After all, food and wine are natural partners.

Tasting with your tongue

Different parts of the tongue register different tastes, so when you take a sip of wine, hold it in your mouth and let the wine roll over your tongue. Professional tasters sometimes swish it around in their mouths like mouthwash, but you may only wish to do this when you are alone! As you hold the wine in your mouth, check its texture. Notice if there is some tartness to the wine (its acidity). Take note of the astringency in a red wine (its tannins)—hopefully it will not be so mouth-puckering that your tongue rebels. Notice if there is a pleasant fruit flavor, maybe several layers of flavors, and a pleasurable aftertaste. These are the hallmarks of a well-made wine.

Temperature affects taste

Another thing that factors into your ability to taste the wine is its temperature. Common mistakes are to serve and drink wine at too cold a temperature for whites and rosés, and too warm a temperature for reds. All wines, even reds, should be served slightly cooler than at modern centrally heated room temperature. When wine is too cold, many of the more subtle flavors and aromas are killed off. When wine is too warm, its alcohol can jump out at you.

A "blind tasting"

A blind wine tasting is one in which you taste several wines without knowing what they are. The wines may be decanted in plain glass containers, or the bottles may be hidden in brown paper bags. The idea is to go one-on-one with the wine, completely free of any preconceived notions about what winery or wine region of the world the wine is from, how much it costs, and even what grape it is made from. Professional tasters often taste wines "blind," and it may be a great deal of fun for you to try it with your friends. (See pages 97–98 for details of how to set up a wine tasting at home.)

Order of precedence

If you are tasting several wines in a short period—at a multi-course dinner, perhaps, or a wine-tasting party —it is wise to drink them in a certain order so your palate is not overwhelmed early on. In general, white wines should be drunk before reds, dry wines before sweet ones, and young wines before older vintages.

Tasting side by side

One of the most helpful tricks in wine tasting, and something professional tasters do all the time, is to taste different wines together. This aids the taster in making comparisons when judging the quality of wines, but to a novice it is especially helpful because you'll learn what you like. Don't know the difference between a Cabernet Sauvignon and a Pinot Noir? Try both side by side and note the real differences in taste, aroma, and body. Think all white wines taste alike? Taste a German Riesling next to a California Chardonnay and you'll never think that again!

Describing what you taste

There is a scientific basis for many of the words used to describe wine. How can a wine smell like grapefruit or taste like eucalyptus? Because wine grapes share many of the naturally occurring chemical compounds found in fruits, flowers, and herbs. An entire body of wine taste-descriptors has been developed (see pages 142–155 for a glossary of wine terms) but, really, anything goes. Any words you can think of that best depict the taste and aroma sensations you get from a wine are helpful in understanding exactly what you like and which bottles you wish to order or purchase next time. So, be creative!

Flavors and aromas in white wines
Let yourself go and explore your senses. The fruit flavors and aromas most often detected in white wines include citrus fruits, such as oranges, grapefruit, lemons, and limes; other soft fruits, like lychees, peaches, and apricots; various tropical fruits, including pineapple and mango; plus gooseberries, apples, figs, and melon. Other flavors often detected in white wines include vanilla, butter or butterscotch, rose petals, nuttiness, and toast.

Highlights of popular whites
In Chardonnay, many people detect apple, banana, and pear aromas and flavors, as well as butter, vanilla, and oak. In Sauvignon Blanc, tasters often identify aromas reminiscent of bell pepper, grass, asparagus, gooseberries, and green beans, along with flavors of grapefruit and other citrus fruits, pineapple, and flowers. In Gewürztraminer, you might note spices, such as clove, cinnamon, or allspice, plus flowery notes, grapefruit, peach, apricot, and lychee flavors. In Rieslings, you could find jasmine, roses and orange blossom, citrus fruits and lemon peel, peach, apricot, pineapple, melon, apple, and honey.

Flavors and aromas in red wines
The most commonly used descriptive words include allusions to various berries—cherry, black cherry,

raspberry, strawberry, blackberry—as well as raisins and vegetal flavors, like green pepper. Other flavors you may find include jam (cooked red or black fruit), black pepper, chocolate, spice, herbs, mint, currant, plum, eucalyptus, anise, tobacco, smoke, leather, and "farmyard" tones.

What can you taste in popular reds?

The answer is a huge range. In Pinot Noir, cherry, mint, anise, vanilla, coffee, soy, and leather are often detected. In Merlot, you might find blackcurrant, blackberry, black cherry, vegetable, herb, and oak flavors. In a Cabernet Sauvignon, tasters often note flavors of raspberry, cassis, green pepper, olives, eucalyptus, mint, black pepper, vanilla, chocolate, coffee, oak, and soy. And in Zinfandel, you could taste smoke, raspberry, and chocolate.

Appreciating older red wines?

Tannins, the astringent and bitter chemical compounds found in grape seeds and skins, help give red wines their aging potential. (They are found in white wines, too, but in much less concentration.) They give off both a flavor and a tactile feeling in your mouth and help preserve the wine over time. Tannins change over that time, too, progressing from young and hard to mellow and soft. So you can actually watch (or taste) your red wine's gradual development over many years. A special delight for wine collectors is to taste a bottle each year from a specially chosen case of a red wine to note how it evolves over time.

Flavors and aromas in dessert wines

The lush, sweet flavors and aromas commonly found in dessert wines include honey and honeysuckle, apricot nectar, orange peel, figs, butterscotch, caramel, ripe and juicy peaches, citrus fruits, and gardenias.

Tasting rosés

Dry rosés, especially those from California and Europe, commonly have red-fruit flavors and aromas such as raspberry, strawberry, and cherry. But since these rosés can be made from grapes as varied as Cabernet Franc, Zinfandel, and Pinot Noir, the flavors and aromas vary widely, too. So-called blush wines, created in California, are sweet, soft, and fruity and commonly contain flavors and aromas of strawberries, watermelon, ripe pear, honeysuckle, and sweet citrus fruits.

Flavors and aromas in sparkling wines

Sparkling wines and Champagnes encompass a variety of taste sensations, from bone-dry and crisp to round and creamy. Flavors and aromas commonly found in sparkling wines include hazelnut, brioche or biscuit, meringue, lemons, apples, figs, pears, citrus fruit, white peaches and nectarines, almonds, licorice, vanilla, caramel, red and black cherries, currants, and strawberries.

Learning more about tasting

As wine consumption grows and new wine regions emerge from around the world, so, too, have wine entertainment and education opportunities. You can further your tasting experiences and deepen your wine knowledge by attending a weekend at a wine "boot camp," a week-long food-and-wine vacation, or simply by dropping into a local wine festival over the weekend. Or give these opportunities as gifts to a wine-loving spouse or parent. Search the Internet or contact wineries, wine societies, cooking schools, or food societies in your area.

how to

5

store wine

As you begin to appreciate wine more deeply, you'll find that you'll want to start collecting a few bottles to keep at home. This makes good sense for several reasons. For instance, you may have found an excellent wine on sale at a bargain price when you buy a case or two. So, if you're not going to drink it immediately, how do you keep it in perfect condition? And how do you choose which wines to keep in order to improve their overall quality and flavor? How long should they be stored? And at what temperature? Is there some mysterious secret to maintaining a wine cellar? Relax! Keeping wine at home, whether it's in a simple storage rack or a fully equipped cellar is no longer the preserve of royalty. Anyone can have a small store of wine at home. Its just a matter of deciding how much you want to keep and what space you have to store it in.

Why store wine?

Okay, let's get real. The average bottle of wine is probably aged about half an hour—between the time you bought it at the store and opened it. And most wines, especially inexpensive and table wines, are meant to be drunk within a year or two. But that said, one of the enjoyable things about some wines is that they keep. Beer and sake (Japanese rice wine) are best drunk fresh, not aged, and this is true for some white wines, too. But other whites, such as Alsace Riesling, white burgundy, and Loire Chenin Blanc, can age five years or longer, and many reds keep for as long as ten or more. They not only keep, they evolve and improve over time. This is what experts mean when they refer to "aging" a wine.

Where to keep it

Whether or not you plan to age it, keep your wine—from one bottle to one thousand—in a dark, cool, vibration-free environment, such as a humid basement, a special wine refrigerator, or a closet. Although many a design magazine features glamorous kitchen makeovers with built-in wine storage among the kitchen cabinets, a kitchen is often the worst place to store wine, because of its fluctuating temperatures and smells.

Not in the refrigerator

The temperature of the average home refrigerator is around 40°F (4°C). You shouldn't drink wines that cold (wines show best at higher temperatures) and it is also too cold for optimum wine storage for the long-term. Most professional cellars employ temperatures from 55–65°F (12–18°C). It is a mistake to store a half-dozen bottles of wine in your refrigerator to drink over many months because you run the risk of harming the wine in the bottles. The refrigerator's constant vibrations can hurt it, and its low humidity level may cause the cork to loosen and the wine to oxidize. (See below.)

The basics of storage

Wine storage systems—whether they are in the form of cabinets, wine racks, or special wine refrigerators—have become stylish status symbols. A multitude of choices is available, ranging from two-bottle stainless-steel racks to one-thousand-bottle mahogany cabinets. But this is sometimes more a question of style than substance. Russian émigré André Tchelistcheff, a chemist-turned-winemaker who influenced the development of the Napa Valley wine industry in the mid-1900s, stored his wine under his bed!

Store the bottle on its side

Why do you always see wine bottles lying on their sides? Because keeping the liquid in the bottle in contact with the cork keeps the cork moist and plump and the bottle sealed. If the cork dries out and allows air into the bottle, the wine is spoiled. For wine you will age for thirty minutes, this is not an issue, but if you have even a few bottles and are not sure when you will drink them, lay them on their sides to ensure they are safe.

Storage temperatures

The best conditions for storing wine involve stable temperatures around 55–65°F (12–18°C), humidity of approximately 80 percent, and darkness—basically, the environment of a cave. Cool temperatures slow the aging process, allowing for better development of the wine over time. Temperature fluctuations cause wine to expand and contract, which can push a cork out and expose the wine to oxygen. This "oxidation" spoils the wine, turning it brownish and giving it a cooked or baked flavor like sherry. Very dry storage conditions may also cause exposure to oxygen.

When darkness falls

Wine stored in darkness retains its clarity. Light reacts to proteins in the wine to form a haze as well as other undesirable effects such as "off" aromas and flavors. Basements and closets (even the spaces under beds) are best for these reasons, and professionally built wine cellars, rooms, and cabinets are all designed to keep your bottles in the dark.

A money-saving investment

Starting a wine collection may sound like a costly proposition, especially if you are a novice or only an occasional drinker. But consider this: collecting, or having an inventory of wines at home, may actually save you money. It'll certainly save you time when you've been invited to a last-minute dinner or you forgot to buy a bottle for your mother's birthday celebration. You can save money by purchasing wine by the case—sometimes even purchasing a half-case will earn you a discount—and taking advantage of sales by stocking up on several bottles. When you buy each bottle you need or want at the last moment from what's available at non-sale prices, you lose both time and money.

Rent or buy?

If there is no suitable place to store wine in your home and you would like to stock up on wine or collect it even on a small scale, you can buy wine storage systems, such as cabinets or refrigerators with insulation and adjustable temperature and humidity controls, or rent lockers or other spaces in warehouses dedicated to storing wine. These should be climate- and humidity-controlled spaces. They are most prevalent in wine-producing regions, but are increasingly available in urban areas, too. Some people with a big wine-collecting habit even use them to hide wine from their spouses!

Storage systems and accessories

If you get well and truly bitten by the wine-collecting bug, you may decide to invest some money in a fully outfitted wine cellar. These can include such equipment as wine racks, refrigeration units, humidifiers, and other accoutrements, and can cost anywhere from a few hundred dollars for a mini-unit wine refrigerator to hundreds of thousands of dollars for a custom-built wine cellar that is an additional room in your home. The bigger and more valuable your wine collection, the more you will want to invest in proper wine storage to protect it. Generally, there are three key elements to effective wine storage at this level: adequate insulation, airtight construction, and an appropriate cooling system.

Wine rooms

Prefabricated wine rooms are usually designed to require assembly at home. There are several manufacturers of walk-in wine rooms, and their products differ only slightly. The types that come with wooden racks for wine bottles are probably preferable to a combination of aluminum and wood wine racks, since they cut down on vibrations. Bottle capacities in wine rooms can range from seven hundred to two and a half thousand plus. These wine storage systems are probably the most cost-effective per bottle of the many choices available.

Wine cabinets

Another wine-storage option is a refrigerated cabinet made of wood or stainless steel that is attractive enough to incorporate into your living space and doesn't have to be hidden in a closet or basement. Cabinets can be freestanding or built in. Manufacturers throughout the world make units that can hold anywhere from fifty to over two thousand bottles. Mini-units with capacities of twenty-four to one hundred bottles can fit beneath your kitchen cabinets or in a wet bar in a living or family room. These claim to protect small wine collections just as well as any larger, more expensive system.

Wine dispensers

Among the many gadgets people with a wine collection find useful is a wine dispenser system. These maintain opened wines for up to three weeks, retarding oxidation, which means they eliminate risk of spoilage. These systems promise "wine storage in a bottle." Used both in homes and at restaurants and bars, the systems preserve the wine with nitrogen and can work for a single bottle or a few cases of wine.

Wine-blending kits

If you want to get more involved with wine, you can even try your hand at making your own blend of wine at home—alone or with a few friends. Merchants sell wine-blending and -tasting kits that contain everything you need to whip up your own unique red-wine blend, just like the pros in Bordeaux. Kits typically include an instruction booklet, glass pipettes, drip stops, blending note sheets, and blind-tasting bottle covers. You can learn the methods used in the Bordeaux tradition of French winemaking—or just enjoy drinking your own concoction.

The best wines to store

It makes sense to store mostly reds because more red wines than white wines improve with age. Tannins, the astringent, bitter group of compounds found in the seeds and skins of grapes, help add to red wine's aging potential (as does acidity) by slowing oxidation. A young wine has new, bitter tannins but after a wine is bottled, the tannins help preserve it and assist the development of increasingly complex flavors and aromas over time.

Wines that improve with keeping

Many Cabernet Sauvignon wines and Bordeaux blends (that usually use Cabernet Sauvignon) continue to improve for ten to fifteen years after the vintage date with proper storage. Pinot Noir and Zinfandel wines can also improve with age—possibly as much as five to ten years after their vintage dates. If you have more than one bottle of the same wine, you might try aging one for a few years, tasting it and then trying the same wine a couple of years later. Even if it's hard to remember what the earlier one tasted like—and this is where keeping notes will help—at least you'll have two pleasurable drinking experiences!

How to start a collection

The problem of knowing how to collect wine deters many people from even starting. So let's make it a little easier for you. Are there particular varieties, say Chardonnay and Merlot, or wine regions of the world that you favor? If so, start a collection with those and move on from there. As you taste and experience wines more fully, you may come up with new categories of your own that you wish to add to your collection. For instance, you could explore New Zealand Sauvignon Blancs, Pinot Noir from around the world, or dry rosés from Mediterranean countries.

What to stock

You needn't have a large or expensive group of wines to call yourself a collector. It's the thought and enthusiasm that count. So while "serious" collectors may invest in extensive ranges of French wines from Bordeaux and Burgundy, California's cult Cabernet Sauvignons, and Italian Super Tuscans, you might just want a handy stock of affordable wines to quaff when friends drop by or to mark an unexpected victory, anniversary, or milestone.

What accoutrements do you need?

If you follow the rules for keeping your wine safe—a dark, cool, stable place—you really don't need much else. People love to get into a subject once they discover its joys, and often this means acquiring paraphernalia. Wine is no exception—but before you start buying grape vintage wall clocks, wine maps, digital hygrometers, and custom-built redwood shelves, remember that you can store wine in the cardboard boxes it came in—as long as you tip them gently on their sides.

Good organization

Organizing your collection properly is a priority for the future. Even if you only have a couple of cases, make a rational plan. Put the wines you'd likely drink sooner rather than later within arm's reach. Stash those worth aging or the seasonal—like summer rosés—behind or below. If your collection is growing, consider an inventory sheet for listing the type of wine, vintage, year purchased, price, and when you want to or should drink it. Computer software is available if you want to get high-tech about it. Make sure your storage place can be illuminated when you need to find something. Wine should rest in the dark, but you shouldn't have to grope your way around a dark basement.

Seeking help

As when ordering wine in a restaurant or buying it in a store, seek out a good merchant for advice on what to stock up on for your home wine inventory. Make sure you can explain your tastes and how often you drink—or would like to drink—reds, whites, rosés, and/or Champagnes, and ask for help in forming a buying plan. This might only mean a few bottles a month, but it will help you organize your thoughts and your wine collection.

How much to buy

Even if budget isn't a great consideration, think about limiting the amount of wine you buy to the amount you can actually drink, entertain with or give as gifts before the wine runs out of steam. In other words, certain types of wine don't last forever. You don't want to get over-excited about a white wine or rosé, buy five cases, drink one, then forget about it for three years. The remaining cases may not be drinkable. Five cases of Cabernet Sauvignon stored properly would have been a safer bet.

Do you even like older wines?

Another thing to consider when deciding what to buy and collect is whether you like aged wines. In addition to experiencing a softening of the astringent tannins of their youth, red wines lose their bold fruitiness with age. Before you invest in a case or two of expensive French or California red wine to age for ten years, buy a few bottles at a store or restaurant and taste them to check whether they suit your fancy. If you don't like the taste, it probably won't much matter to you how they have "evolved" over time.

how to

6

serve wine

Serving wine correctly is an art in itself. Whether you're having a casual get-together with friends or a more formal wine and dinner party, you can add that extra touch of pleasure to the occasion just by knowing how to prepare, serve and pour wine properly, using the right types of wine glasses, and gauging the correct temperature for the type of wine you are serving. All this ensures that you and your guests get the very best from every bottle. These are not trivial matters—for instance, the temperature at which a wine is served has an immense impact on its flavor. It's also useful to know how to decant wine, not just for aesthetic purposes, but also to allow the wine to breathe, and improve its flavor. As for what glasses to use, you don't have to spend a fortune on fine crystal—just choose a few basic shapes, and keep them sparkling clean, so that they enhance the delicious flavor of the wine you're enjoying.

Setting up a wine bar at home

If you've never done it before, setting up a wine bar in your own home can be great fun. Depending on how big your gathering is, you may want to set up one or more wine bars in different rooms of the house. These can be pour-it-yourself areas and should contain everything a bartender needs to serve wine or wine drinks: several bottles of several types of wine, an ice bucket or two for the wines that should be chilled, some bottled water (still and sparkling), a corkscrew, towel, and wine glasses. Invite guests to help themselves as you greet them and remind them to refill their glasses as the evening progresses.

What gadgets do you need?

Not many. Although you could go crazy with wine paraphernalia—and you may have some fun with it—you need not buy a lot of gadgets to serve wine to guests, whether you're entertaining a couple of friends or a party for fifty people. The essentials: wine, of course, plus wine glasses, Champagne flutes, a corkscrew, a wine bucket for chilling through the evening, a decanter if you need to decant a wine, and at least a few nibbles to complement the wine.

Friendly help

If you have plenty of cash to hire a professional bartender for an extra- large party, that's fine. Otherwise, it's down to you or a helpful friend. At a sit-down dinner, it is supposed to be the host's job to pour the wine around the table and to make sure glasses stay filled. But do you really need to stand on such ceremony at your parties? Rules of etiquette aside, if it's a big occasion, you may want to ask a friend or two to fulfill this duty so that you can be sure no one goes thirsty and you can attend to other details.

The finer points of wine serving

Don't fill the glass too much because guests, if they want to, cannot swirl wine if the level is too high. (See pages 58–59 for the benefits of swirling and sniffing before tasting.) It's best to fill them about one-third full to leave plenty of room in the bowl. Some people pour wine until it reaches the widest part of the bowl, well below the rim. Remember, glasses can always be refilled—and refilled!

How to pour the wine

As they do in restaurants, always try to pour the wine with the label pointing toward your guests so people can see what they are drinking. To guard against red wine drips on your light-colored tablecloth or a friend's delicate silk clothing, use "drip stops" or wine-savers: small, round, laminated paper disks stuck into the mouth of the bottle, which make any drips that form roll back into the bottle. Or try fabric-lined rings that sit around the top of the bottle to catch any wine that rolls down the side. Then there is the "twist-of-the-wrist" style of pouring in which you twist the bottle slightly as you pull it up and away from the glass you are filling. Waiters and *sommeliers* sometimes prefer to hold the bottle by the "punt," or indentation, at the bottom of many bottles. If you find that it makes pouring easier, do it. Practice makes perfect!

Holding the glass

Set a good example for the other guests by holding your wine glass by the stem, not the bowl. This is not a wine-snob affectation: It makes very good sense. If your fingertips smudge the glass, you see the color of the wine less clearly and it looks less appetizing. If your hands touch or cup the bowl, the wine warms up from your body heat faster than you can sip it.

Order of service

Due to the way chemicals affect human senses, there are some guidelines to follow about the order in which you should serve and drink different wines. Generally, drink dry wines before sweet ones because sugar stays on your palate and affects the taste of what comes afterward, making dry wines sour and bland-tasting. Drink lighter wines before heavier ones for the same reason: Full-bodied, full-flavored wines dilute the flavors of lighter wines.

Old before young

Young wines are usually more fruity, intense, and tannic than older wines and overpower them if drunk first. Maturity—and the complexity and depth that comes with it—rates over the callow young wine that hits you over the head. Don't overwhelm taste buds with strong flavors that compromise your experience of older, more rare wine.

Open in advance

To avoid last-minute problems and scrambling, open all your wine bottles about ten to fifteen minutes before your friends arrive. This way your bottle-opening skills (or lack of them) will not be on display. You will also feel better knowing the job is done before they even walk in the door.

Cork-removal gadgets

Many vintners and wine-drinkers prefer the traditional cork in the wine bottle and wouldn't think of selling or buying a bottle with anything else. They seem attached to that trademark popping of the cork pulled from the bottle. The range of corkscrews available attests to this, from simple, inexpensive devices that require the user to put some muscle into the process to high-tech, high-cost models that do most of the work for you.

The "waiter's friend"

The original "waiter's friend" corkscrew is inexpensive and a favorite of waiters and wine servers around the world—so it must be good! It has a plated metal handle and a fold-out screw in the middle with a small knife to cut the foil capsule at the top of the bottle. At one end of the handle is a two-inch/5cm fulcrum that pulls out and extracts the cork. Watch your waiter use this corkscrew or ask for a lesson next time you have the opportunity.

Other types of corkscrews

Once you start looking, you'll find that there are many types of corkscrews. Ask for one that does not have screws that are too large because they can shred the cork. It should not push loose corks down into the bottle, such as the two-pronged "Ah-so." Or seek out one that does all the work for you, if that is what you prefer, such as the winged corkscrew. The simplest model is a plastic screwpull that is small, cheap, and works very well.

Dealing with corks

It can be really annoying when a cork breaks off in the process of removing it from the bottle, but you shouldn't worry about it. Just take the broken part out of the neck of the bottle and reinsert a corkscrew into the remaining piece. If this doesn't work and the cork falls further down the bottle or into the wine, again, don't get into a state. If it has been properly stored, the cork has been in contact with the wine for months and presents no problem to the wine's taste or quality. If you do not finish the bottle, you will need to find an alternative method of closure that will keep the bottle airtight until you do. Do not allow wine remaining in the bottle to sit open for any length of time, such as overnight, or it will be ruined.

Reinserting the cork

The best way to store wine is to push the original cork back in the bottle with a fairly tight seal, though not so far that you need a corkscrew to open it a second time. You can purchase cans of nitrogen and other gadgets to prevent wine changing for the worse overnight. However, many are no more effective for a couple of days than simply stopping the bottle with its own cork.

Champagne corks

Never try using a traditional corkscrew for opening a Champagne bottle. To open Champagne, remove the outer foil at the top of the bottle and hold the bottle at a forty-five-degree angle away from you, your guests, and anything breakable or valuable. Untwist the wire cage around the cork. Hold the cork and slowly twist the bottle, not the cork, until the pressure inside the bottle pushes the cork out slowly. Ideally, you hear a "phsst" sound as the trapped carbon dioxide gas is released.

Screwcaps

Although it has no romance, and is still in the experimental stage, many in the wine industry say there are advantages to a screwcap over natural cork. The wine lasts longer and there is no possibility of cork taint—a musty, wet-cardboard taste and smell imparted to the wine when the cork goes bad. Screwcaps are widely used in Australia, where they are said to be better at retaining fresh, fruity flavors of white wines such as Chenin Blanc, Riesling, and Gewürztraminer because of their tight seal that allows no oxygen into the bottle. Another advantage is that screwcap bottles do not need to be stored on their sides. The jury is still out, on the matter, though, because screwcaps haven't been used long enough to prove that they allow for good long-term aging.

Old wines and their corks

When you're about to open an old wine, look to see if there is any mold on the cork before you open it. If so, wipe it away and, after removing the cork, check for any mold residue or pieces of cork left on the rim of the bottle after opening it and wipe the lip of the bottle with a damp cloth. If you are drinking a very old wine with a lead capsule, wipe away any lead residue before pouring the wine. This step really depends on the wine, and is not necessary with most of the wines you will drink.

Decanting wine

You may decant wines into a glass container for several reasons. An older wine can lose most of its sediment in the decanting process; a young, tannic red wine will soften from being exposed to oxygen, or you may simply want to use that beautiful antique decanter your grandmother handed down. One hint: if you have guests who care, keep the bottle so they can see what they are drinking.

How to decant

Although decanting wine sounds really easy, it should always be done very carefully. If the bottle contains sediment and the purpose in decanting is to lose the sediment (which is harmless, by the way), make sure it has been sitting upright for at least several hours, allowing the sediment to settle at the bottom. While opening the bottle, take care not to shake the contents. Make sure the decanter is not smaller than the bottle, or you will be stuck with extra wine in the bottle and no place to put it. Pour the wine in one firm, continuous flow into the decanter in a well-lit area so you can watch the wine flowing out. When you see the first bit of sediment trickle into the bottle's neck, stop pouring immediately.

Other reasons to decant

There are other practical reasons to transfer wine from its bottle to a glass carafe, such as if the bottle was already opened, maybe from earlier in the day or the night before, and you don't want friends to think they are being served "leftover" wine, or if the label has gotten wet and fallen off the bottle, or you want to have guests taste the wine "blind" (See page 98 for organizing blind tastings.)

Wine glasses

Make sure glasses are spotless. This means cleaning them by hand, not in the dishwasher (where they run a greater risk of breaking). Wash them thoroughly, one at a time, so they won't break in a crowded sink. Don't air dry glasses, which can lead to spots or streaks. Instead, set them upside down on a soft, thick towel to let water slide off. Then dry by hand. Make sure no soap residue is left behind.

Cleaning tools

There are special washing brushes for stemware and decanters designed to access those hard-to-reach places where red wines sometimes leave a sticky film. (Alternatively, add a little bleach and water to the glass or decanter and let sit for a few minutes.) There are also drying racks for decanters and wines glasses. Cleaning liquids specially formulated for glassware that cut grease, butter, olive oil, fingerprints, and lipstick are helpful, too. Makers claim they won't etch, pit, or cloud your stemware.

Wine only, please

Don't use wineglasses for any other purpose—iced coffee or tea, parfaits or ice cream. They may look attractive in the glasses, but you may never rid stemware of the smells of dairy products nor remove the cast of coffee or tea.

Grandma's cut crystal?

Although the wine industry would like you to use clear glassware so you can better admire its handiwork, the bottom line has to be your personal enjoyment. If you adore the cobalt-blue wine goblets you received at your wedding, or have a special attachment to the heavy, cut-crystal goblets your grandmother handed down, by all means use them for drinking wine (but sparingly, as lead crystal reacts with wine and releases lead into your system every time you drink). Maybe you won't see the color or clarity of the wine as much, but you'll probably enjoy it all the more because of the good feelings you get from your most precious objects.

What kind of glasses?

Remember, when you're purchasing new glassware, that it's best to have thin, not thick, glasses. A thin rim feels more comfortable on your lips and transports the wine more smoothly. Smooth, clear glass is better at displaying a wine's color and clarity than chunky, colored glass, etched glass, or glass with patterns on it.

Size and shape

The shape and size of the glass can also affect the way a wine tastes. Today's makers of fine glassware claim their designs release the fullest aroma of each grape variety based on the shape of the bowl and the corresponding width of the rim. Or, they say, the shape of the glass directs the wine to certain places on the tongue and captures the bouquet, enhancing the pleasures of each wine. Usually, each glass they sell is designed for a particular type of wine, the better to enhance its bouquet and taste. Wine-glass designs are the result of thousands of years of glassmaking trial and error.

Special glasses for different wines?

Many wine connoisseurs follow the theories above and invest in pricey glassware. But if you don't swallow it, or can't afford to invest in a set of fine glassware for each type of wine you are partial to, simply purchase a set of high-quality, all-purpose glasses with a capacity from eight to fourteen ounces. An all-purpose wine glass is suitable for white, red, sparkling, and dessert wines and is easily available everywhere from department to discount stores.

Red-wine glasses

The so-called balloon shape with a rounded bowl is the most common shape of glass recommended for red wine. Because each wine has different amounts of components, such as acid, sugar, tannins, and chemical compounds, different glass shapes manipulate your experience of drinking the wines they hold. The "science" behind which shape is associated with which wine is a trial-and-error experience, but the glassware companies have done the experimentation for you. Serve Bordeaux blends, Cabernet Sauvignon, Pinot Noir, Merlot, and Zinfandel in these.

White-wine glasses

The so-called tulip shape is the most common shape of glass for white wine, its shape determined best to deliver the particular weight and components of white (and also rosé) wines to your mouth. You should serve white wines such as Sauvignon Blanc, Chardonnay, Riesling, Pinot Gris, Pinot Blanc, and White Zinfandel in these glasses.

Champagne glasses

The *de rigueur* Champagne glass used to be a round, broad, shallow glass or metal cup (modeled on Marie Antoinette's breasts, the legend goes), but today's undisputed ideal for sparkling wine is a tall, narrow flute that allows the bubbles to have a nice long float all the way to the top of the glass. Serve Italian spumante or Prosecco, French Champagne, Spanish cava, sparkling wine, and German Sekt in these glasses.

Dessert wine glasses

Dessert-wine glasses come in different shapes—some tulip shaped, others like smaller Champagne flutes—but they are usually smaller than those used for dinner wines. There are "scientific" reasons for their design, as with any wine-glass shape, but there is a practical reason, too; at the end of a meal, most people tend to drink quite a bit less of a dense, rich dessert wine than they do dinner wines. Serve Auslese, ice wine, late-harvest Gewürztraminer, and Sauternes in dessert-wine glasses.

Arranging glasses on the table

If you have more than one wine at a dinner party and want to provide multiple glasses, the best way to place glasses on the table is in the order they will be used, right to left. The water glass sits farthest right above the knife.

Why more than one glass?

It's not so common today to have a different glass for every wine, but there are good reasons to do so. With two glasses, your guests won't feel obligated to finish one wine before they try another. Also, some diners may want to compare two wines or to try both the red and the white wine with the fish course.

How many glasses?

For large parties, plan to put out two glasses for every one guest. This is so your friends can have a clean glass should they misplace the one they were drinking from, or change to a new glass if they've switched from drinking red to white wines, or so you can quickly and graciously provide a friend with a new glass should one break. Consider renting wine glasses from a party-supply service.

Serving temperatures

What they say about wine temperature is true—it really does matter. Serving temperature has an important effect on what you taste when you bring the glass to your lips; some experts say it's the most important effect. When a red wine is too warm and a white wine too cold (the most common mistakes involving temperature, encountered even in fine restaurants), the wine will not taste its best. At lower temperatures, aromas are lessened and this cuts down on your enjoyment of the wine.

Red-wine temperatures

The custom followed in most countries is to serve reds at room temperature. However, current opinion in the United States says red wines are actually best enjoyed slightly cooler than modern room temperature. Massive, tannic red wines are best served at the high end of a scale of 55–70°F (12–21°C); lighter wines, such as Beaujolais, Pinot Noir, Sangiovese, and Chianti, sit at the lower end. So, to cool your red wine, put the bottle in the refrigerator or ice bucket, if only for ten to thirty minutes.

White-wine temperatures

White wines need to be chilled, but not too much. An easy rule of thumb is thirty minutes in the freezer or one to two hours in the refrigerator. If you've had a bottle in the refrigerator for several days, take it out fifteen to thirty minutes before serving. Sherry, Chardonnay, Meursault, and

Montrachet will display more aroma, have richer flavor, and better feel in the mouth at 55–60°F—warmer than lighter or fruitier dry whites, such as Riesling, Sauvignon Blanc, Muscat, Chenin Blanc, Viognier, and Muscadet, which are best when served at 50–55°F.

Dessert- and sparkling-wine temperatures

Sweeter, dessert, late-harvest wines, and all Champagnes can take the coldest temperatures of all: 45–55°F (6–12°C).

Gauging temperature

So what are you supposed to do: take the temperature of a glass of wine before serving it? Believe it or not, wine thermometers do exist—even one with an alarm that goes off when the wine in the bottle reaches the desired temperature! Another type wraps a heat-sensitive cuff around the bottle and tells you the wine's temperature. If gauging a wine's temperature this way seems tedious, use these simple rules: A bottle of red should feel cool to the touch, but not cold. If too cool, leave at room temperature for thirty minutes or so. If too warm, refrigerate for thirty minutes. Serve a white wine straight from the refrigerator in warmer months. Let it sit for fifteen minutes in winter.

Quick chill

To chill a bottle quickly, fill a bucket with ice and water and put the bottle in it for fifteen to thirty minutes. Make sure the bottle is taking a complete ice-water bath. Remove before serving, or it will continue to chill. To keep white wine chilled after removing it from the refrigerator, fill a bucket with ice and rest the bottle on top of the ice.

wine for all

7

occasions

Wine is brilliantly versatile, as fitting for a snazzy occasion, like a fiftieth anniversary party, as it is supper for two. It goes down nicely at a tailgate party, a formal dinner, or a late-night tête-à-tête. Big, small, noisy, quiet, understated, or flashy—any type of gathering can showcase the many pleasures of wine. The key to success is knowing which wines suit the occasion—whether it's a large-scale graduation or birthday celebration, an outdoor picnic, or a romantic Valentine breakfast. Don't assume that entertaining with wine is prohibitively expensive. Just take a look at what's on offer. As more wine regions open up their treasures to the world, there's an amazing array of choice, and you'll find something delicious to suit a modest budget. Hosting a wine-tasting party is a novel "learning with fun" event that combines several pleasures. It's fun, intriguing, a great experience—and helps to deepen your appreciation of wine even more.

Basic calculations

A general rule of thumb is one bottle of wine for every two people at a gathering. At a drinks party or a mix-and-mingle party, it might be more, since typically there is less attention on the food being served and less time and fanfare taken in serving it—thus more time spent sipping. If you have ten friends coming, plan on at least five or more bottles of wine. Adjust this formula for friends you know will want to escape the grape and imbibe cocktails instead, or for those who don't drink much and will nurse one glass throughout the evening.

How much for a sit-down dinner?

For a sit-down dinner, stick to the one-bottle-for-every-two-people rule, but adjust it for non-drinkers, those who might want to continue their cocktails during dinner, and also those among your guests who will stick to white (or red) throughout dinner, even though you offer different wines with different courses. Also, in the spirit of being a generous host, it's always best to have a bottle or two extra than to be a bottle or two short.

Keep your guests in mind

Your budget need not be the only sensible consideration when deciding what to spend on the wine for your party. Whether your wines come from Chile (the lower-priced end of the fine-wine scale) or Bordeaux (the upper end) might also depend on the friends you are inviting. If they are wine novices, an expensive California "cult wine" or a Mouton-Rothschild would probably be lost on them, and you might not get any reaction—or satisfaction—for your efforts. So always keep the wine-appreciation level of your guests in mind and save the Mouton-Rothschild for a friend who will truly appreciate it.

Value for money

In today's climate, with wine regions burgeoning throughout the world and offering competitive prices, there really is no need to spend a lavish amount of money on quality wine. Once you determine the number of guests, the amount of wine you need, and the budget for your party or occasion, you can assess how much money you can spend on wine. Again, seek the advice of a wine merchant—whether at a fine-wine store or a discount beverage warehouse—and clue him or her in on your budget. If it's on the high side, your vendor might recommend Bordeaux or Napa Valley wines. If you're watching the pennies, your best bet may be Australian or Chilean wines. Either way, you and your guests are bound to be satisfied.

Wines for every occasion

Big milestones, such as weddings, anniversaries, New Year parties, certain birthdays, and graduations call for festive wines. This almost always means Champagne. It may also mean special wines like Bordeaux blends or Cabernet Sauvignon that people often save and age for special celebrations and once-in-a-lifetime occasions. Or it can mean any wine you especially enjoy or one that your guest of honor favors.

Romantic breakfast

Morning is usually a bit too early to indulge in straight wine drinking, so the best drinks to serve before noon are wines or Champagnes mixed or diluted with other liquids. For instance, a traditional favorite served with breakfast or brunch in New Orleans, Louisiana, a culinary and celebration center of the United States, is a Mimosa, made of Champagne and orange juice.

Christmas holidays

Use your imagination and think pink when you are choosing wines for the Christmas holiday table. Although they are most often touted as summer wines, dry rosés make excellent accompaniments to a Christmas turkey dinner, New Year's ham, or the pâtés, cheeses, and breads of holiday party buffets. Rosés and pink sparkling wines, with their colors ranging from rich cranberry to pale salmon, look good on the holiday table, too. Dry rosés are made in France, other Mediterranean countries (Spain and Italy), and throughout California.

For an evening in

For sheer wrap around pleasure, try a comforting red in winter, especially on a rainy or snowy evening. A velvety Pinot Noir can certainly do the trick, as can a Sangiovese from Italy, a spicy Syrah from California or France, or a Shiraz from Australia. These are all wines that aren't too powerful to drink alone and also go well with food. In warmer weather, a spicy Viognier, a light Riesling, or a Pinot Gris can accompany everything from popcorn and a DVD to a home-cooked meal.

For instant cheer

Champagne will certainly do the trick. It is usually labeled as a "special-occasion beverage." This means that most people think of it as suitable only for those few particularly celebratory times in life, such as weddings, engagements, and christenings. Consequently, they feel excessive or indulgent if they drink it at other times. But with its effervescence, its delicate color and crisp taste, Champagne is irresistibly mood-boosting. For modest budgets, try Spanish cava, German Sekt, Italian spumante and Prosecco, and American and Australian sparkling wines.

Birthdays and anniversaries

The most important thing is to make sure that that the guests of honor get to enjoy the wines they love the most. If your birthday boy is a Cabernet-lover, you might get a great bottle for the party and another as a gift to save. Or, if the lady adores bubbly and it's a big party serve up the Champagne—maybe even several different kinds.

Perfect for picnics

Warm weather inspires thoughts of picnics, barbecues, and alfresco dining. Which wine is best at these sometimes portable summer feasts? The ideal wines for casual summer repasts fall into three groups: dry rosés; fruity whites, such as Viognier and Pinot Grigio; and powerful reds, like Sangiovese and Rhône varieties (such as Syrah or Grenache). These full-bodied reds tend to have lots of fruit. All these wines tend to be reasonably priced, too.

A Valentine's treat

You might want the traditional Champagne in an ice bucket for a romantic dinner for two. But for something different (or if there's no romance in your life at present), try a red-wine-and-chocolate-tasting as a Valentine's treat for you and your friends. As odd as it may sound, red wine and chocolate complement each other wonderfully, and it is delightful and illuminating to taste the way the sweetness of the chocolate softens and enhances the fruit of the red wine. First, bite into the chocolate or taste a small spoonful of chocolate syrup, and coat your mouth with it. Then take a sip of red wine. Delicious.

For après ski

When the snow has been dusted from your hair and fatigue has settled into your bones after a long day of skiing, you probably want a mellow wine like a Merlot, a Syrah, or an older Cabernet Sauvignon: wines that will calm and soothe you after your workout. You might find these wines more comforting than those that require heavy chilling, such as Champagne or fruity whites, which you might want to save for picnics and other summer outdoor events.

For summer outdoor grilling

Classic American barbecue fare—grilled steaks, hamburgers, chicken, and vegetables brushed with olive oil—goes well with wine. Use the same food-and-wine pairing rules you'd use at any occasion (see Chapter 8, pages 104–15 for the details). Even in the United States, not exactly a wine culture on par with many European countries, the idea that wine is only for fancy food is outdated. So introduce wine to your backyard!

Business lunch or dinner

It's worth knowing that your wine savvy, or lack of it, can actively help or hurt you in a business setting. Nowadays, wine is considered to be such an integral part of business entertaining that there are extracurricular clubs and activities at the world's top business schools focused entirely on wine tasting and education. It's very much a sign of the times. Just as one had to play golf in times past to succeed in some fields of business, you now have to know how to order wine with confidence. The way you handle selecting, ordering, and drinking wine can make a significant impression on a professional colleague or a prospective boss. And that's why it's important to demonstrate that you're a real wine aficionado. The day of the three-Martini lunch may be over, but the business lunch or dinner with wine is very much with us. (See pages 20–24 for how to order wine.)

Note: Wine may be a genteel beverage, but it is important to remember it is still alcohol. Too much of a good thing (and wine is one) can still be a bad thing. Festive occasions and special celebrations are often about excess, but you really don't want to let the alcohol consumption at your parties get out of hand and spoil the occasion.

Hosting a wine tasting party

An organized wine tasting with friends can be great fun, introducing an extra, educational dimension to getting together. Tasting wines side by side is the most effective way to learn about wines, to understand what you like best, and to compare the attributes and quality of different wines. So try hosting a wine-tasting party or suggest that a friend who's interested in wine (and has more wine glasses than you do) hosts it.

How to organize the tasting

You organize a tasting in terms of "flights" of wine—two or more related wines. They can be related in several ways: by grape variety—three Chardonnays, for example, one from each of three different countries; by region—three South African reds; or by producer—four Zinfandels from the same winery covering different vineyards, different vintages, or different blends. Or try three Merlots, one each from three very different price categories. Be creative and organize your tasting according to what you'd like to experience.

What do you need?

Each taster should have three glasses if you are tasting three wines, four if you are tasting four, and so on. Make sure the glasses are clean and have no smell. Use a white tablecloth so you can best see the color of the wines. Have a small pad of paper and a pencil or pen next to each place setting so tasters can take notes if they want to. Things to take note of include the color, smell, and taste of the different wines. Encourage the tasters to share their observations.

Tasting "blind"

Adding an element of surprise can make the wine tasting even more fun. Pour a small amount of wine—about a third of the glass capacity—in each glass without identifying the wines. You can simply announce that the wines are all Pinot Noirs, or all from California, or all rosés from European countries. Mask their identities by wrapping the bottles in small paper bags and number them, or pour them into carafes (this is trickier to number—use tape—and you have to make sure you keep straight what you poured into each carafe). Pour wine number one in the first glass on the right in front of each taster, wine number two in the second, and so on. After everyone has tasted their wines and discussed them, try guessing what is what or from where. At the end, reveal the identities of the wines. You can even reward the person who has the most correct guesses (even among experts, they are often guesses) with a bottle of wine to take home.

Is it polite to spit?

Yes, it is at a wine tasting. You or your guests may squirm at this idea at first, but professional tasters use spittoons or cups at a tasting event to avoid swallowing all the wine. For them, it is a necessity, since they often taste as many as fifty or more wines at a sitting. But even if you are sipping from just four or five different glasses, you might not want to swallow it all. Provide ceramic jars or Styrofoam cups for your friends at a tasting so guests needn't swallow everything they taste (also very important for those guests who are driving home). They can ignore them if they like, but you will probably find that once you all get over your initial shyness about spitting, they will come in handy.

Single-focus tasting

Vary the recipe for a wine tasting by having a comparative tasting of only one kind of wine. For instance, you might decide to taste Spanish sherries, or ports, or Champagnes. Do not worry about not having four sherry glasses available per person—who does nowadays? Use wine goblets or ask your friends to bring their own glasses, ones they will drink from throughout the evening. Since these drinks can be expensive, you could also ask each person to bring a bottle. After you've finished the wine tasting, encourage everyone to take home what is left in their bottle, since everything but the Champagne has a reasonable shelf life.

Wine-tasting groups

If you and your friends have enjoyed a wine tasting, it might evolve into a wine-tasting group. Some people belong to book clubs, others to cooking clubs; wine-tasting groups work much along the same lines. Members of a group of friends or acquaintances rotate as hosts for the tasting, so everyone gets a chance. The tasting might take place as often as once a month or as infrequently as twice a year, whatever works best for your schedules.

Quick and easy parties

You want to get together with a group of friends, have a bonding session with your work colleagues, or throw a housewarming party. But time is short. The easiest recipe for this is a wine-and-cheese-party, since everything can be bought (wine, cheese, bread, crackers, fruit) and nothing needs to be cooked. One way to organize such a party is to pair each cheese with a wine from the same country or region the cheese comes from: for example, a French Roquefort with a white burgundy, a Spanish Manchego with a Tempranillo or a California Chardonnay with a Sonoma goat cheese.

Dessert party

This is really easy to set up—and it's also highly enjoyable, especially if you have friends who adore desserts. After a movie, play or concert, invite friends back to your place for a luxurious spread of desserts. Again, everything can be purchased at a bakery or grocery store or made by you ahead of time. Here, wine can play a starring role. Sauternes, late-harvest dessert wines, port, and Champagne are all delicious with an array of desserts from dense, rich chocolate tortes to lighter fruit desserts. Include a cheese plate, too, and don't forget the coffee and tea.

Spring brunch

Host a spring brunch at the first sign of sunny weather. In addition to breakfast items, serve light-lunch dishes including quiche or frittata, salads, chilled marinated asparagus spears, crudités, and a fresh-fruit salad. Chilled Champagne, mimosas, a light white wine such as a Riesling and/or a rosé would all work well with most brunch items. Provide sparkling water for those who might like to mix it, or alternate it, with their wine.

Wine and hors d'oeuvres party

People lead busy lives, so having a classic "cocktail" party when you don't feel like hosting a dinner or you and some friends are going to a concert or a play later in the evening makes sense. Serving wine instead of cocktails means no preparation or mixing so you can enjoy the party instead of playing bartender. This also encourages people to meet each other, since no one is stuck next to only a few others for the duration of the meal. All your friends can meet each other more easily.

Serve a selection of wines with a selection of finger foods you can buy, make, or heat up from frozen. If you serve enough finger foods and some of them are hearty fare, they can even serve as a dinner substitute. Set up a wine bar or two (include water bottles, soda, and ice at these) around your home and food tables so you do not have to serve guests all night. Start passing around hot hors d'oeuvres when about half of your guests have arrived, replacing the dishes often. Also serve several varieties of cold hors d'oeuvres that won't need your attention after being set out.

Handling a formal dinner party

When you're pulling out the stops, you should serve different wines with different courses at a formal dinner party. If your meal has three courses and you will have three different wines, make sure you have three glasses for each person. (Borrow from friends if you don't have enough or rent wine glasses for the evening from a party service.) The table should be set with the three glasses, plus a glass for water, at the beginning of the meal. Pour each glass one-third full, introducing the new wine as you serve each course. Don't have all three glasses already poured when your friends sit down to dinner. Leave the bottles on view so people can see what they are drinking and can help themselves to more, unless you are acting as pourer, or a designated friend take on that role. (For advice on which wines to serve with each course, see the following chapter on food-and-wine matching on pages 104–15.)

Wine makes a perfect gift

If you're not giving the party yourself, but have been invited to it, you may decide to take along a special bottle of wine for your host or hostess. To highlight the fact that you are presenting the bottle as a gift (rather than as a bottle to be opened and enjoyed that evening), you might say something like, "This is for you to enjoy later," or "This is specially for your cellar." When you're choosing the wine to take along, pick one that matches the recipient's tastes, interests, and level of wine knowledge. For instance, you might select a fine Cabernet Sauvignon for a Cabernet-lover. If your host or hostess is planning to go to France on vacation, why not bring a bottle of excellent French wine that will celebrate the adventure ahead? If you're not familiar with your host or hostess's personal preferences, it's a safer bet to select a classic wine variety, such as Chardonnay or Merlot.

Choosing a special bottle

Why not encourage people to share your pleasure and join the growing community of wine aficionados? For special occasions, such as milestone anniversaries, end-of-the-year holidays, or to please a long-standing client, a hard-to-buy-for mother, or a wonderful son-in-law, spend some time selecting an appropriate wine to give as a gift. Ask yourself whether your recipient is likely to open the bottle immediately or age it in a cellar or wine closet. If the latter, ask at the wine store for a bottle that will age well. Will the wine be brought out to wow friends at a dinner party? You might consider an impressive, large-format bottle. Does your friend have a favorite wine or a wine-country region? If so, cater to that whim. If you buy direct from a winery, it's usually possible to buy a bottle signed by the winemaker or winery owner.

Presenting wine

A well-chosen wine is always received with pleasure, whether taken along to drink at a dinner party or presented as a birthday gift. And gifts of wine no longer need to come in a plain brown wrapper. In fact it can be very attractively packaged now there are so many innovative options available in store. Look for beautiful and unusual paper wine bags available in supermarkets, winery gift shops, and fine-wine stores. If you want to think outside the bag, consider more unusual packaging, such as a planter, a canvas tote bag, or an inexpensive wine bucket. If it's a gift for a wine aficionado, you might want to accompany the bottle with some quirky wine gadgets, such as drip stoppers, an innovative corkscrew, or wine charms.

wine

8

with food

Are some wine and food partnerships truly made in heaven? Well, yes—some are. Strawberries and Champagne are a perfect example, and the classic combination of Muscadet and moules marinières really do seem made for each other. So, it's often a good idea to pay attention to established tradition, as well as learning to explore your own taste preferences. This will give you the confidence to experiment, and the knowledge of when to ignore mainstream recommendations. Most people tell you that you should drink red wine with red meat—but try serving a young, fruity red with roasted chicken, and you'll soon discover how quickly that rule is disproved. You'll find it's a great combination. As a useful rule of thumb, pair sweet wine with sweet food, acidic wine with acidic or salty food, spicy wine with spicy food, red wine with red meat and white wine with white—that way, you'll always be safe.

The basic guidelines

Have you heard the familiar cliché about always drinking red wine with meat and white wine with fish or chicken? Who hasn't? And should you take any notice of it? These days it's regarded as an outmoded idea, since white wines and red wines of very different styles can often be enjoyed quite nicely with the same dish (roasted chicken is a perfect example). The bottom line is that you should drink the wines you enjoy most with the foods you like best, regardless of color. So why worry at all about what wine goes with what food? Well, both wine and food are complex substances with taste elements in them that can be altered depending on what you're combining in the same bite. So there are quite a few legitimate considerations when pairing wine with food that will considerably heighten your enjoyment of both.

Light vs. heavy

While its fine to kick against some preconceived ideas about wine, there are some rules to keep in mind. When pairing wine with food, lighter wines go better with lighter foods and heavier, full-bodied wines go better with richer, heartier cuisine. Drink a light white wine like a Riesling or a Pinot Grigio or a light red wine like a Pinot Noir with a light dish like pasta primavera. But beware—not all Pinot Noirs are light! The point is that a delicate white wine that would go well with a delicate seafood dish such as Coquilles St. Jacques would be overwhelmed by a slab of beef. If you love White Zinfandel, but want to have prime rib for dinner, try having your White Zin as an aperitif and have a glass of (or a sip of your friend's) heartier red, such as a Syrah or a Merlot, with your beef. Start with this notion when choosing a wine for your food—or when choosing the food to go with the wine you'd like to drink.

Simple vs. complicated

Another basic rule that some people like to follow that may make a lot of sense to you, is the one about complexity. The more complicated the flavors in the food, the simpler the wine. For example, a New Orleans-style gumbo with lots of different ingredients, spices, and flavors is best paired with a young red wine, not an old Cabernet Sauvignon revealing layer upon layer of flavors (although most experts agree that beer is the best partner for this dish). Instead, save that old Cabernet for a flavorful cheese, simple crackers or nuts, or even to drink alone. That said, rules are meant to be broken, so experiment and try different combinations.

Look to the origins

Another useful general rule in pairing food with wines is to look to the region where your food or wine comes from and pair accordingly. Pair a southern Italian red wine with a seafood dish from southern Italy. Combine a Sancerre or Sauvignon Blanc with a classic French preparation of seafood, such as *fruits de mer*. Match a strong cheese from Greece with a Greek wine, or a grape variety that came from Greece. The idea is that these recipes and wines grew up together, so to speak, and probably adapted to each other over time, so they are a safe choice. You may find this rule too restrictive or impossible to follow, but when in doubt, it's a useful notion to keep in mind.

Rich foods

Red wines pair well with fat-rich foods, such as different cuts of beef, because of the wine's tannins—the thing that preserves the wine and allows it to age. So do crisp, dry Champagnes—their acidity cuts through the super-rich tastes of liver pâté, *foie gras*, or deep-fried foods.

Seasonal foods

You may want to think of wines as "seasonal" in the same way that foods are. Pinot Noir goes well with lamb and mint for spring. Chardonnay is a summer wine that pairs well with the foods of summer, such as fresh fruits and vegetables. Deep and rich Zinfandel goes well with the heartier foods we veer toward as the weather turns cool in fall (and is often touted as perfect with turkey for Thanksgiving dinner). And for winter, sparkling wine takes center stage at holiday parties and occasions, but also pairs well with the rich, comforting foods of winter, such as mushrooms.

What doesn't go with wine?

Any combination you don't like! Wine, though a versatile, elegant, and delicious beverage, doesn't always hit the spot for all people. Don't feel forced to drink or serve wine at every fancy occasion or with every food you serve. Wine experts and writers will tell you that wine goes with everything from borscht to wild boar, but don't always believe it! Here are a few foods that you may find wine doesn't match terribly well: pickles, vinegar, asparagus, celery, candy, ice cream, cookies, cream cheese, peanut butter, and popcorn.

Using wine in your cooking

What would a hearty spaghetti sauce be without a dash of a robust red wine? Or *coquilles St. Jacques* without the addition of dry vermouth? Or a creamy cheese fondue without a splash of white wine? Wine adds great flavor to your cooking and is not complicated to use in many dishes. It's as simple as adding a splash of sherry or Madeira to your homemade chicken or turkey gravy, or adding ¼ cup of dry red wine to spaghetti sauces, stews, and many hearty Italian dishes such as chicken *cacciatore*. Steam mussels and clams in a mixture of white wine and water, and poach scallops and salmon in a poaching liquid of dry white wine or vermouth, water, spices and other flavorings, such as carrots and celery. You needn't be a gourmet cook or a cooking-school graduate to get creative with wine.

What to buy for cooking

The wine industry will tell you never to use any type of wine in cooking that you would not drink straight, but that is overzealous advice based on wanting, as in any business, to sell as much of its product as possible. Instead, let common sense guide you. Using an entire bottle of very expensive red wine for "drunken pork" (in which pork marinates overnight in the wine, which is then discarded) or a high-end white burgundy to steam clams or mussels is a waste, and an unnecessary drain on your budget. On the other hand, if you only need one-third of a cup of wine for your recipe and want to drink the rest of the bottle with the meal, it might make sense. Don't buy cheap, so-called "cooking wines" in the grocery store, because the quality and taste will not do justice to your culinary efforts. But feel free to buy at the lower end of the price scale when searching for a bottle that you will use primarily in a recipe—as long as you stick to known quality wines. After all, you may want to finish off the bottle after you've used what you need in your recipe. The wine should be good enough for that!

Cook with it, drink it

When your recipe calls for wine and you're also going to serve wine with the meal, choose the same type of wine to serve. That doesn't mean the same bottle, because it makes more sense to spend more on the wine you will drink. But you still want compatibility between the wine in your dish (especially if there is a lot of wine in it, such as in *coq au vin*) and the wine you will drink along with it. So serve a pricier Zinfandel at the table if you are putting Zinfandel in your *coq au vin*. By the way, most recipes will simply call for a "dry red wine" or an "off-dry white wine," in which case feel free to choose a wine within that category that suits your taste and budget.

Getting the right food-wine match

When you want to order a certain dish but have an inkling your favorite wine will be too subtle or overpowering with it, seek the advice of the server or *sommelier,* if there is one. Describe the kind of wines you like and then explain your food choice. Since servers or *sommeliers* should be familiar with the ingredients in various dishes on the menu, they should be able to come up with suitable suggestions, and you can expand your horizons by trying a new wine or a new combination of food and wine. If a new wine you've never tasted is suggested and you're not sure about ordering it, ask for a small taste. (See pages 26–35 for food-pairing suggestions listed by wine types.)

Wines with chicken

When you're choosing wines to go well with chicken dishes think about what ingredients have been used in the recipe. They can vary immensely. Heavier wines, usually reds, would go well with a hearty chicken cacciatore (containing spices, tomatoes, and other vegetables) while a light red wine, such as Pinot Noir, a light white, such as Sauvignon Blanc, or a dry rosé would go well with plain roasted chicken. Chardonnay, a light red wine, or a fruity Viognier goes well with a smokier-tasting grilled chicken or chicken with a fruity sauce.

Which wine goes with beef?

Again, to choose a wine for beef you must consider how the beef is prepared. If it's a plain, juicy steak or a slab of prime rib, a robust wine such as a Cabernet Sauvignon, Zinfandel, Syrah, or Bordeaux blend would stand up to it and help cut the fat that will coat your mouth. For an Italian dish that contains beef but also flavorful ingredients like garlic, tomatoes, olives or cheese, try an Italian red, California Zinfandel, Cabernet Sauvignon or Merlot, or a Shiraz from Australia. Cabernet Sauvignon and Syrah (Shiraz) go with a variety of grilled red meats and stews. Merlot is ideal with winter stews and hamburgers. Cabernet also matches well with heavier meat dishes, such as sausages and beef-and-bean dishes. Sausages and ribs also go well with Zinfandel.

Wine and other meats

Pinot Noir, one of the most food-friendly of all wines, is compatible with pork, duck, lamb, venison, and wild game, although many people prefer heartier, powerful reds with the last four meats; try Napa Cabernet, Rhône reds, or Australian Shiraz. For a roast lamb with garlic, olive oil, and other pungent Mediterranean flavors, try Italian wines, Zinfandels, Cabernet Sauvignon, or Merlot. A rich, oaky Chardonnay also drinks well with a light meat, such as pork or squab, but make sure the sauce or accompaniments aren't too strongly flavored.

Choosing wine with fish

Sauvignon Blanc (Sancerre in France) complements lighter fish dishes, such as shrimp, crab, lobster, Petrale or Dover sole, and halibut. Chardonnay, generally richer than Sauvignon Blanc, goes well with richer fish or fish dishes, such as grilled salmon, shrimp scampi, and Lobster

Newburg or lightly spiced fish dishes. Pinot Noir also pairs well with salmon; Merlot works with tuna and swordfish.

Wine with oysters?

Why a tip on matching wine with oysters? Because there's at least one major competition dedicated to the subject each year. And raw oysters, with their pure, briny taste of the sea, combined with a crisp white wine is a sublime combination. At the Pacific Coast Oyster Wine Competition, an annual contest to identify a group of wines that can be recommended as good "oyster wines," the wines chosen as best paired with oysters on the half-shell are usually Sauvignon Blanc (or French Sancerre), dry Chenin Blanc (or French Vouvray), and Pinot Gris. Other excellent choices are Muscadet, Chablis, and dry Riesling.

Matching wine with pasta

All pastas have basically the same taste, so you need to concentrate on how a pasta dish is sauced to match it best with a wine. Is it light or heavy? If it's a delicate olive oil and/or butter sauce with a hint of garlic and parsley, drink a Pinot Grigio or other light white wine or a light red. If it's a hearty sauce packed with vegetables and meat, go for a Sangiovese, a Tuscan blend, a Chianti, or a Zinfandel.

Wine and snack foods

Champagne with potato chips? Yes! The salt and oil of the chips is a perfect contrast to the crisp acid of a dry Champagne. Light, crisp sparkling wines usually contain fresh, fruity flavors that refresh and cleanse the taste buds when eating salty, creamy or nutty foods, so instead of saving the bubbles only for special occasions, think of it for your casual snacks, too. Pizza is great with many red wines—Sangiovese, Chianti, Cabernet Sauvignon, Merlot—

and some whites such as Pinot Gris and Chardonnay. Salted nuts and olives go with just about anything light and young, such as Merlot, Chardonnay, or Pinot Grigio. Sherry is always served with little dishes of salted almonds, olives, and other tapas in Spain.

Which wine with Japanese food?

The Japanese would say *sake* (rice wine) goes best with Japanese food, but the western world has found that sparkling wine is a perfect match for *sushi* and *sashimi* (delicate raw fish slices without the vinegared rice). Because of its subtle flavors, it will not overwhelm the subtle taste of the fish, and its high acid content will tame the fire of the green horseradish (*wasabi*) and ginger slices that accompany it. Pinot Grigio or Sauvignon Blanc would go well with raw fish, too. Deep-fried shrimp, chicken, or vegetable tempura would also match well with sparkling wine. For the sweet-salty flavors of *teriyaki* chicken or beef, try Cabernet Sauvignon, Merlot or a Bordeaux blend.

Choosing wine with salads

Matching salads with wines can be tricky because of the vinegar in most salad dressings. If you can substitute lemon juice for the vinegar in your salad dressing, you can avoid the clash of flavors that results from wine and vinegar. Creamy salad dressings are another answer, allowing you to choose freely what wine you drink. But watch out for particularly bitter salad greens, such as arugula or radicchio, which can clash with wines. Choose a wine high in acidity, such as a Sancerre (Sauvignon Blanc).

Which wine with desserts?

That's easy: the classic dessert wines. Sauternes, late-harvest wines, port, and Champagne all go well with certain desserts. Also, port and chocolate are an amazingly good match, and many dessert wines are a good partner to lighter, fruit desserts.

Do dessert wines seem like too much?

Even many people who are devoted wine-drinkers say enough is enough and often turn up their noses at dessert wines by the end of a meal. They may feel they have had too much alcohol, too many calories, or that the sweetness of the dessert wines is too much for them combined with the sweetness of the dessert they're eating. If that's the case with you, feel free to forgo a port or a late-harvest wine at the end of the meal. Or, you might want to try the dessert wine instead of dessert, since both are sweet.

Wine and chocolate?

Here's a surprising combination: Cabernet Sauvignon with chocolate. For those who normally regard a full-bodied Cabernet Sauvignon as too robust or harsh for their taste buds, the chocolate is a perfect antidote. The sweetness of the chocolate softens and enhances the red wine and brings out its yummy fruit. First, bite into the chocolate, then take a, perhaps tentative, sip of red wine. You'll be pleasantly surprised at what you experience.

Matching wine with vegetarian cuisine

Vegetarian diets are increasing in popularity, and even non-vegetarians eat more salad, bread, and vegetables in a typical meal than they do an entrée of meat, poultry, or fish. So it is surprising that more attention does not get paid to pairing wine with vegetarian cuisine. Wine can go beautifully with vegetables, cheese, breads, pulses, and other side dishes or staples of a meat-free diet. Just adopt the following rules:

Light vs. heavy

We're back to the light and heavy rule. Pair a heavy wine such as Cabernet Sauvignon with robust, starchy vegetables like fresh corn or roasted potatoes, and they will bring out the fruit in the wine. A stuffed artichoke or roasted vegetables with olive oil will also go well with a Cabernet Sauvignon because the roasted quality of the vegetables complements the darker tones of the Cabernet. The same wine would also work well with a hearty vegetarian lasagne.

Compare and contrast

A crisp Sauvignon Blanc or Chardonnay matches well with a creamy soup, such as sweet corn or cream of mushroom. A fruity white wine could also provide an interesting contrast to the creamy texture of an artichoke. Pair fruity, bright wines, such as Sauvignon Blanc or an Italian red Sangiovese, with vegetables that have bright flavors, such as tomatoes, asparagus, and green beans.

Go rustic

Earthier wines go well with rustic foods like grilled potatoes, red peppers, and olives. Cabernet Sauvignon can work well with bean dishes and strong cheeses. Provençal reds, such as Bandol, or Italian Sangiovese are nice with a rustic, whole-wheat olive bread or something similar. A Zinfandel would enhance savory dishes that include berries or fruits, bringing out the wine's jam characteristics. And Merlot always goes well with a vegetarian pizza.

the world's

9

wine regions

Today, drinking wine is like going on a world trip without leaving home. Never before has so much wine, in such variety, been exported from so many countries on such a scale. We are now living in a golden age of winemaking. Just look at the shelves of your local wine store, and check out the places where the wine was made. Then you'll realize the sheer scale of what the world's wine regions have to offer. You can sample wines from regions as far apart as Australia and Argentina, Chile and Spain, California and Bordeaux, often at easily affordable prices. Moreover, travel companies have zeroed in on wine lovers preferences, and offer tours to wine-producing regions, with trips to wineries and wine tastings included as part of the package. That's when you'll really appreciate drinking local wines and brews with the local cuisine. Here is an armchair traveler's guide to the key wine-making locations to start whetting your appetite.

FRANCE

Classifying French wines

Don't be confused by French wines with unfamiliar names. Here's everything you need to know: In France, wines are not named or classified by grape variety, as "New World" wines are (those from North America, Australia, New Zealand, South America, and South Africa.) So, just when you've learned to differentiate a Pinot Noir from a Pinot Gris, you'll find it of no help when reading a French wine label. French wines are named sometimes by the geographical areas from which they come (Bordeaux, Burgundy, Rhône) and often by even more specific regions and *appellations contrôlées* (official classifications) within those areas. There is also a complicated system of classifying wine based on quality. In Bordeaux, for instance, the 150-year-old system of rating wine estates put in place by wine merchants even varies from one region within Bordeaux to another. These top wines are *crus classés*, or "classified growths." *Premiers crus*, or "first growths," are the top classified wines, the most prestigious and pricey. There are *deuxièmes crus*, "second growths," etc., all the way to fifth growths. You'll also find *premier-* and *grand-cru* vineyards in Burgundy (e.g. for Chablis).

Know your terminology

Château wines are French wines produced by a wine producer who owns a château. The word originally meant "castle" or "big house", but today, what it really means is the kind of winery that has vineyards and/or a wine-making facility on the property. Yet far from the grandeur that the word suggests, the facility and building could be quite modest. The Bordeaux region has the most, but not the only, châteaux, and wines made by, say, Château

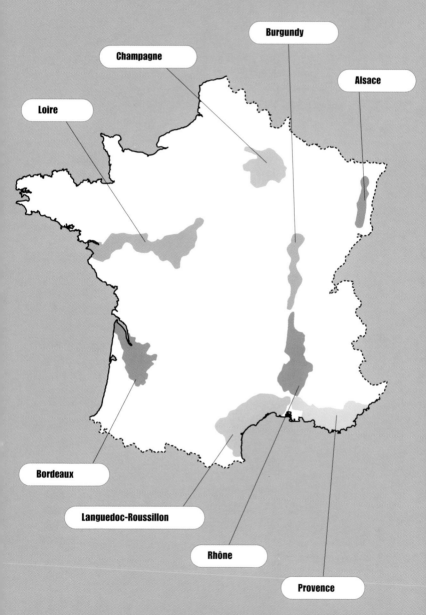

Burgundy

Champagne

Alsace

Loire

Bordeaux

Languedoc-Roussillon

Rhône

Provence

Margaux and Château Lafite are among the world's most revered. Today, however, many wine producers in France (and all over the world, including the U.S.) have tacked the title "chateau" onto their names—the better to sell wines.

The Bordeaux region

If you can, you should visit Bordeaux—it is considered one of the best wine regions in the world—and buy Bordeaux wines, known for their finesse and high quality. Nobody does it like the French, and Bordeaux, located in southwest France, is the most famous fine-wine region in the world. Bordeaux's reds are usually based on Cabernet Sauvignon and Merlot, but almost all are blends, including other varieties, such as Malbec, Cabernet Franc, and Petit Verdot. Good Bordeaux rouge (red) is crisp, herbal, and cedary, with blackberry and blackcurrant flavors. The Bordeaux region also turns out Sauternes, one of the most famous dessert wines. Most Bordeaux wines are expensive and highly prized because they age for a long time. Top areas include Margaux, Pauillac, Pomerol, and St-Emilion. Lesser known but good regions within Bordeaux include Puisseguin St-Emilion, Blaye, and Lalande de Pomerol.

The Rhône

If the venerable Bordeaux and Burgundy regions seem a bit too much like the wines mother or even grandmother might prefer, try France's Rhône region for something a little more trendy. Grenache, Syrah, Mourvédre, Cinsault, and Carignan are the main varieties produced in this region, located in the south of France, near Provence. The highest-quality wines, ones that are rich-tasting, high in alcohol, and loaded with fruit, are from Châteauneuf-du-Pape and Gigondas in the southern Rhône. Wines from the Côtes du Rhône can be good buys and are generally drunk young. In the northern Rhône, Côte-Rôtie and Hermitage are known for their steep hillside vineyards that grow Syrah, a spicy red (although whites are produced as well).

Burgundy

Burgundy is known for its expensive wines, complex Chardonnays and Pinot Noirs that are often cited as the best of their kind in the world. Whereas most white wines should be drunk within two to three years, white burgundies with their multi-layered flavors, can age for five years or more as they develop deeper aromas and flavors. Top Burgundy areas include Chablis, the Côte de Nuits, and the Côte de Beaune. The highest-quality level of wine, and most expensive, from Burgundy is the *grand cru*. The lowest is a Bourgogne (red or white), but many wines at this level are well worth trying and provide good value for money.

The Loire

Visit the Loire in central France for an easy, laid-back wine-country weekend while visiting Paris. And if you like crisp, dry white wines from the Chenin Blanc, Sauvignon Blanc, and Muscadet grapes, Loire wines will tickle your fancy. Not quite on a par with Burgundy or Bordeaux, the Loire region still produces desirable wines. The best-known are from the Vouvray, Sancerre, and Pouilly-Fumé appellations. Rosé d'Anjou is one to watch. The Loire is France's second-largest area of sparkling-wine production.

Languedoc-Roussillon

Try the so-called Rhône varieties from the Languedoc-Roussillon, France's most up-and-coming wine region. Value, dynamism, and excitement—this area has it all. Once the source of ordinary table wines, the Languedoc is the largest French wine-producing area and offers reasonably priced Chardonnay, Merlot, and Sauvignon Blanc (often called by their grape variety names—unusual in France) and new, high-quality Rhône wines made from Grenache, Mourvédre, Carignan, and Syrah grapes by a band of devoted artisan makers with ambitions to build the area a higher profile. Some of the best wines come from Faugères, Pic St-Loup, and Coteaux du Languedoc.

Champagne

If you love Champagne, then why not go to the source? Legendary around the world as the birthplace of the wine world's most festive product, Champagne in northern France is one of the world's coolest winemaking regions. Champagne from Champagne is about traditions dating back to the seventeenth century, and is made using the same three grapes—Chardonnay, Pinot Noir, and Pinot Meunier—sometimes as a blend of two or all three, sometimes as 100 percent Chardonnay (*blanc de blancs*). It is always made using the *méthode champenoise*, or Champagne method that developed here. It undergoes two fermentations, the second giving those tiny bubbles. Champagne can age, but most people prefer it young while it still has a lively kick. It also makes great cocktails.

Provence

Head for Provence—or a wine store—for dry rosés. Known more for its bewitching ambience than its wine, this green region in southern France, sprinkled with medieval hill towns, underwent a change after enjoying international literary limelight in the 1990s. As in most of France, wine has been made here for hundreds of years, but it was lackluster. Now, quality has improved. The area, especially Lubéron, provides tourist tours, tastings, and even a corkscrew museum. Wines are pleasantly affordable.

ITALY

You might say (especially if you're Italian) that Italians like and know wine better than anyone else in the world. That's because Italy makes more wine than any other country and its people rank third in consumption per capita. There are wine-growing regions all over the "boot" and on its principal islands, and Italy's intricate wine regions are notorious for their complexity. The country has experienced a dramatic rebirth of its winemaking since the 1990s. There are a striking variety of wines made here—from the enigmatic and expensive "Super Tuscans" to a wide variety of respectable table wines that certainly won't break the bank. Barbera, Nebbiolo, Dolcetto, Montepulciano, and Sangiovese are Italy's most common and popular red grapes; Pinot Grigio its best-known white.

Piedmont

Choose the mighty Barolo and Barbaresco wines that hail from the Nebbiolo grape in Piedmont if you want rich, powerful wines. Among the highest in the hierarchy of Italian wines, wines from this region of northwest Italy also include Barbera, "the people's wine," that goes down easier than most wines made from Nebbiolo. Dolcetto is another easy-drinking red. Among dry whites, the most common and highly favored is Arneis, followed by Favorita. Piedmont is known for Asti, a sweet-ish sparkler.

Tuscany

Experience Tuscany for yourself, either in person or in a glass of its most emblematic grape, the Sangiovese. Set in central Italy's bucolic countryside, Tuscany is one of the prime winemaking regions of the world. Dotted with ancient olive trees, old vines on rolling hills of green velvet, and medieval villages, Tuscany is also one of the best wine

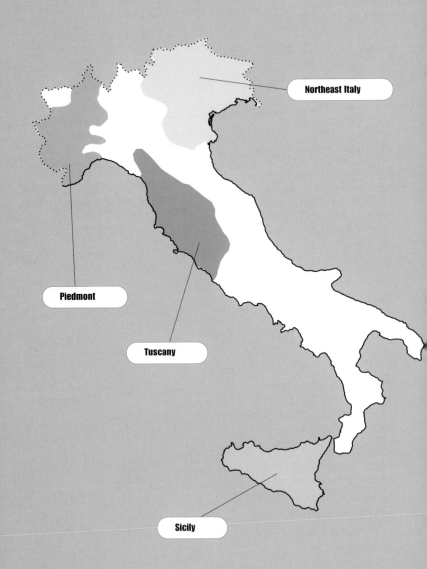

Northeast Italy

Piedmont

Tuscany

Sicily

regions to visit,with its famously beautiful landscape and historic cities such as Florence. This is the home of Chianti, that familiar wine-in-a-basket; it also gave birth to the "Super Tuscan" and high-quality reds with long names, like Brunello di Montalcino and Vino Nobile di Montepulciano. Dry whites made here come from the Trebbiano grape, although the finest are almost all Chardonnay these days.

What is a Super Tuscan?

A group of ambitious Italian wine producers from Tuscany created the so-called "Super Tuscan" in order to promote a new type of wine that would improve the region's reputation. They aimed to make wine with international appeal. That's why they decided not only to use the native grape of Tuscany, Sangiovese (sometimes 100 percent), but also "international" grape varieties like Cabernet Sauvignon and Merlot in blends. Super Tuscans, as the name suggests, are big, bold wines that can happily stand up to rich, flavorful foods. The winemakers' aspirations were fully realized. These are expensive, prize-winning wines made with care—and it shows.

Northeastern Italy

There is sufficient variety of wines to please most people in this area north of Tuscany and east of Piedmont—a diverse region responsible for some of Italy's most popular wines. Northeastern Italy encompasses the wine regions of the Veneto, Friuli-Venezia Giulia, and Trentino-Alto Adige. The choice is impressive—ranging from the more familiar wines, such as Cabernet Sauvignon, Merlot, Chardonnay, Gewürztraminer, and Sauvignon Blanc, to native Italian wines, such as powerful red Amarones, fruity Pinot Grigios, crisp Soaves, and the fizzy white Prosecco; there is sure to be something for everyone here.

SPAIN AND PORTUGAL

SPAIN

Among European wine cultures, the first to spring to mind may be France and Italy, but Spain comes a close third. Although it is the third largest producer of wine in the world, Spain has more grapevines than any other country, and its roots as a wine culture extend across thousands of years. Wine is a staple at mealtimes, and Spanish art and religion is infused with images of the grape. There are seven major wine regions scattered throughout Spain, and Tempranillo, a robust red grape, is the best-known Spanish wine outside the country. Many wineries in Spain, known as *bodegas*, are open for tours and tasting.

Rioja

To experience royalty, try Rioja wines. They are made mostly from a blend of the intensely flavored Tempranillo grape (usually 60–70 percent), Garnacha (Grenache, 15–20 percent), and the rest made up of Graciano and Mazuelo grapes. This fairly small area in the northern part of the country is the king of Spain's winegrowing regions—and one of the world's great wine-producing areas. Located in north-central Spain, Rioja is a pleasant and delicious diversion from Spain's crowded tourist meccas. Travel here and you'll find the locals take great interest in food, wine, and conviviality—often until the wee hours.

Priorato

For cutting edge Spanish wines, try wines from this up-and-coming Spanish wine area. Priorato is a small wine-producing area about 90 minutes's drive west of Barcelona. Thanks to some remarkable wines made by a small group of makers, who dubbed themselves "crazy romantics" to be

PORTUGAL

Rioja

SPAIN

Penedès

Porto (capital of the
port-making region)

Jerez

Priorato

Ribera del Duero

making wine in such rugged, steep terrain, Priorato has garnered notice for its new-style red wines that are rich, full-bodied, fruity, and complex.

Penedès

If you like your bubbly, especially at reasonable prices, try Spanish cava from the world-famous center of the cava industry. The Penedès region, less than an hour's drive from the dynamic, daring city of Barcelona in Catalonia, has been making sparkling white from three grapes native to the region for hundreds of years. It is a Catalonian tradition especially popular in European countries. Some impressive still wines come from the Penedès area, too.

Jerez

For something a little different from reds and sparkling, try Fino sherry from the place it originated. Sherry is *the* aperitif in Spain, and a great partner for *tapas*, the delectable appetizers that can make up a whole meal. Sherry, invented in Jerez, southwest Spain, was imitated all over the world, but true sherry comes only from Jerez, where a certain kind of yeast, *flor*, gives the unique flavor.

Ribera del Duero

If you like concentrated, fruity red wines, you will really like the wines from this wine region in north-central Spain west of Rioja. Ribera del Duero is home to one of the country's most prestigious wineries and is a great place to visit any time of year because of its outstanding natural beauty. Most of the red wines are made from Spain's mighty Tempranillo grape (known here as Tinto del País), but bodegas also blend Tempranillo with Cabernet Sauvignon, Malbec, Merlot, and Garnacha, to achieve a more fashionable, international style.

PORTUGAL

Look to Portugal, located southwest of Spain, for its eponymous product, port, and some respectable dry table wines—quite light, low in alcohol, and perfect for midday drinking over a long lunch. Port is a fortified wine with smooth, aromatic flavors. Most ports, dark and rich, should not be drunk for ten to twenty years after bottling, but few loyal port fans probably wait that long. (White port, a treat rarely found outside the country, makes a refreshing, early-drinking aperitif when served over ice.) A bottle of port isn't cheap, but this is a slow-sipping, after-dinner wine, one that lasts for a long time and doesn't go bad after opening—brandy added to the wine stabilizes it for a long life. Madeira, named after the Portuguese island it comes from, is another fortified wine.

GERMANY AND AUSTRIA

GERMANY

Remember this next time you're staring at a confusing German wine label with a long, unpronounceable name: Germany makes some of the best wines in the world, especially whites. Don't be scared off! The complicated ranking system of German wines, along with those indecipherable names, have left many consumers scratching their heads and moving on to a Pinot Gris from France or a Pinot Grigio from Italy. Its greatest wine areas include the Mosel river valley, the Rheingau, Rheinhessen, and the Pfalz, and its greatest grape is the Riesling.

German rankings

Tafelwein (table wine) is the lowest quality level of wine in Germany. *Qualitätswein bestimmte Anbaugebiete* (thankfully shortened as Q.b.A.) is a step higher and classifies the mid-

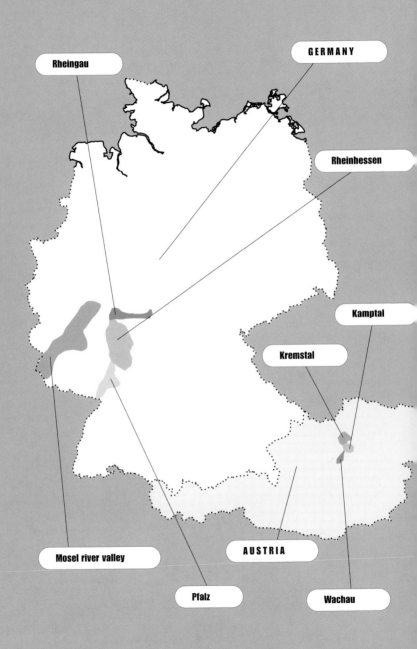

Rheingau

GERMANY

Rheinhessen

Kamptal

Kremstal

Mosel river valley

Pfalz

AUSTRIA

Wachau

level German wines, while *Qualitätswein mit Prädikat* (shortened as Q.m.P.) is the next, and highest, quality level of German wine.

AUSTRIA

Austria, famous for its music scene, is often overlooked when it comes to wine, but do not commit the same error! Top wine producing areas in this landlocked country south of Germany include the Wachau, Kremstal, and Kamptal. Austria's fresh and fruity white wines, such as Grüner Veltliner and Riesling, are the standouts of the country, but it also makes respectable red wines, such as Blaufränkisch and Zweigelt, with deep berry flavors. Austria is also renowned for its dessert wines. The top whites and dessert wines are the most expensive, but there are good value whites and reds.

UNITED STATES AND CANADA

THE UNITED STATES

Every state in the fifty that make up the U.S. has at least one winery. The regions that dominate American wine are California, Washington State, Oregon, and New York State. California produces 90 percent of all U.S. wine. If it were a nation, it would be the fourth leading wine-producing country in the world, behind France, Italy, and Spain.

The Napa valley

The 1976 Paris tasting was a historic moment in the wine world: French and American wines—with their identities hidden—were judged by professional French tasters. The winners in each category were wines from the Napa Valley. It was the first time in history that American wines had won out over French ones in a formal setting, and it shocked

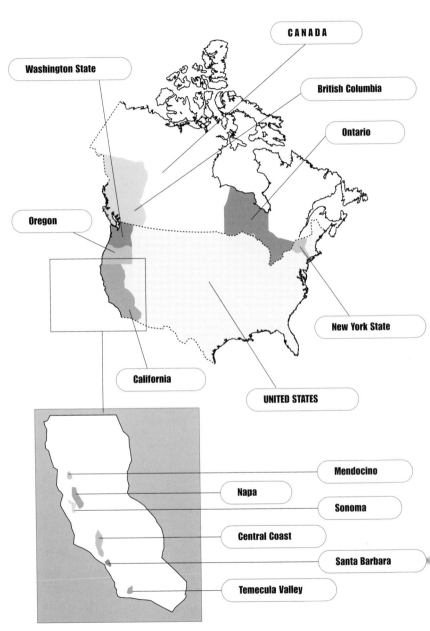

CANADA

Washington State

British Columbia

Ontario

Oregon

New York State

California

UNITED STATES

Mendocino

Napa

Sonoma

Central Coast

Santa Barbara

Temecula Valley

both the French and the Americans. From this point on, Napa became known as the little valley that could. This relatively small, narrow valley is now the United States' best-known wine region, even though it produces only a minute portion of the state's wine output. If a wine region had a personality, Napa would be driven and straight-laced: the kid in the class who always strove to be the best. American wine pioneer Robert Mondavi established his winery here in the 1960s and tirelessly promoted Napa Valley and American wines around the world. The climate, soils, and grape farming and winemaking talent contribute to making Napa Valley wines world-class. Cabernet Sauvignon is the main attraction and the highest-priced wine, but Chardonnay, Sauvignon Blanc, Zinfandel, and Merlot grape varieties are also widely planted and the wine they produce is rated highly.

Top-dollar for top-drawer

If you have a taste for Napa Valley Cabernet Sauvignons, shop smart. They are generally many times the average price for a bottle of wine from the rest of the state. For reasonably priced Cabernets from the region, avoid labels marked "Single Vineyard" or "Estate Bottled." Instead, look for wines that say "Napa Valley" or "Napa County." Older, more established wineries often sell their wines at lower prices than small or new boutique wineries.

Laid-back Sonoma

If Napa is like a black-tie dinner, Sonoma, its friendly next-door neighbor, is more a frat party. As long ago as 1872, this was the number-one wine producer in the U.S., surpassing Los Angeles, the California industry's birthplace. Today, Sonoma has four major grape-producing valleys and is much bigger and more diverse than Napa. It has always lagged behind Napa in promoting its wines, but they are generally on a par with Napa wines in quality, while most sport lower price tags. Sonoma's Pinot Noir from the cool Russian River Valley and Zinfandel from warmer regions are among its better wines.

Mendocino

When you're in for a bit of a bohemian adventure, try wines from colorful Mendocino, a beautiful coastal area north of Sonoma and Napa, long overshadowed by its more famous winemaking neighbors. Locals, who might answer to "Sunshine" or "Rainbow," even invented their own language to keep outsiders at bay, and more than a few grow crops that aren't quite legal, especially in more isolated inland areas. But the Anderson Valley, close to the cooling effects of the Pacific Ocean and therefore ideal for sparkling wine, Chardonnay, and Pinot Noir, puts out wines that compete with the best anywhere. Some wineries also make excellent Zinfandel, Sauvignon Blanc, and Gewürztraminer. Because of its dramatic coastline and laid-back atmosphere, the region is great for a visit.

California's Central Coast

Shop California Central Coast wines if you're looking for really good value. The Central Coast of California used to be known as the "vast nothingness" situated between San Francisco and Los Angeles. Now, the Monterey and San Luis Obispo areas are reputable wine-producers, with lower prices than most Napa and Sonoma wine. The coastal location means Chardonnay and Pinot Noir, two grape types that benefit from cool weather and coastal mists, thrive. In the Paso Robles area, Sauvignon Blanc, Syrah, and Cabernet Sauvignon do well. Look out for wines from the Edna Valley.

Santa Barbara

You'll want to try the area's Chardonnay and Pinot Noir, since this is a coastal area just north of Los Angeles that benefits from cooler weather, and is kind to those two cool-climate grapes. Other wines that are Santa Barbara success stories include Rhône varieties, such as Grenache, Syrah, and Viognier. Missionaries first brought grapevines to bucolic Santa Barbara county in southern California in the 1770s. But for the past hundred years it's been known more for Gucci than Grenache because of its reputation as a playground for the Hollywood rich. Today, the area encompasses two dynamic wine-growing regions —the dominant Santa Maria Valley and its smaller colleague, the Santa Ynez Valley—and over seventy wineries.

Temecula Valley

Try the respectable to very good wines made here with lower price tags than many other areas of California. The Temecula Valley is a small wine-country region of vine-yards, ranches, and foothills one hour from Los Angeles and San Diego. The region was hard-hit in the late 1990s by a pest that destroyed about a third of its vineyards. Although California's first grapes were planted here by Spanish missionaries some 200 years ago, most wineries are fairly new. Wines to look out for include Cabernet Sauvignon plus interesting white Viognier and Pinot Gris.

Oregon

Pinot Noir is the star wine of this state. When Bob Dylan wrote "A hard rain is gonna fall!" he was probably in Oregon wine country. Unfortunately, when the clouds let loose during the fall harvest, it can jeopardize the entire area's wine output—thus the quality of Oregon wines varies from year to year more than its neighbor to the north,

Washington, and its southern neighbor, California. Yet when the harvest is good, Oregon wines are excellent. Besides a multitude of delicious Pinot Noirs, Cabernet Sauvignon and Merlot are worth trying. For white-lovers, taste Pinot Gris, rapidly becoming an Oregon specialty.

New York State

It's only a cottage industry, but vintners from New York's Long Island, which juts out into the Atlantic ocean, are making some of the state's best wines—wines that are commanding the attention and the allegiance of some of New York City's most high-toned restaurants. The Long Island wine industry boasts a maritime climate and mild winters. A few dozen vintners have planted grapevines in former potato fields, with very good results. Chardonnay, Merlot, rosé, and sparkling wines are all worth trying. A considerably older wine industry dating to the early 1800s is located upstate in the Finger Lakes region, which turns out some delicate dry white wines, such as Riesling, plus dessert and ice wines. In the 1990s, the Finger Lakes area experienced a boom in boutique wineries.

CANADA

British Columbia

Canada's wine regions have it all: open landscapes, plentiful sunshine for ripening grapes to their optimum, high-quality wines, and great value due to favorable exchange rates. Some of the leading high-quality wines produced in the Okanagan Valley, one of Canada's two major wine regions, include aromatic and delicate white wines such as Riesling and Pinot Blanc. In British Columbia, many European immigrants to the south of Okanagan have developed vineyards and wineries in a climate similar to that of the north of France. Within a 150-mile range, marked with blue-and-white "Wine Route" highway signs, there are about forty wineries, with free tours and wine tastings. There are wine biking tours and major wine festivals.

Ontario

If you are an ice-wine devotee, look to Ontario, the other high-quality wine area that has emerged in Canada. Even some French vintners are buying wineries and producing wine here. Notable wines include Cabernet Sauvignon and Merlot, along with whites such as Gewürztraminer, Chardonnay, Riesling, and Pinot Blanc. But the star product of this area is ice wine, made principally in the Ontario region due to its consistently cold climate. This dessert wine is deep and rich in aroma and flavor. Canada exports about 15 percent of its wine to foreign markets, including the United Kingdom, Japan, China, and the United States, so you do not have to visit to enjoy them.

THE SOUTHERN HEMISPHERE

AUSTRALIA

Look to Australian wines for big statements. The country's trademark wines are its generally inky Shiraz (Aussie talk for the French Syrah) and oily Chardonnay; the Australian way is to make them powerful and highly flavored. Australian wines have assaulted the world marketplace with high-quality products at reasonable prices. Its group of winemakers—an adventurous, experimental lot—have been found soaking up the wine culture everywhere from France to Napa and taking what they learn back home. This huge, dynamic country has a handful of expansive wine regions and produces an amount of wine that is growing at

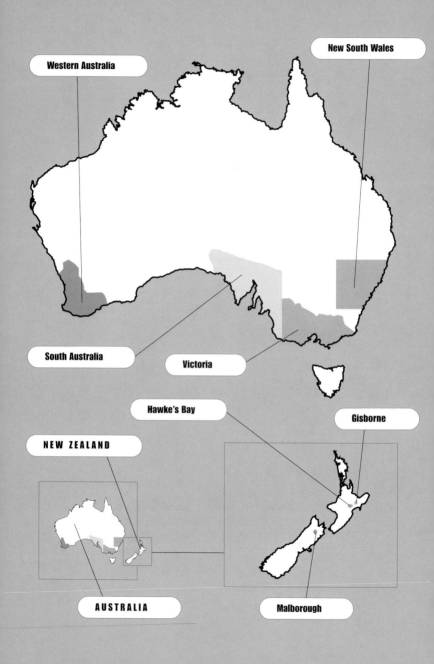

Western Australia

New South Wales

South Australia

Victoria

Hawke's Bay

Gisborne

NEW ZEALAND

Malborough

AUSTRALIA

phenomenal rates due in no small part to their good value. An up-and-coming wine to look out for from Australia is another French grape variety: Grenache.

Notable areas

The major wine-producing regions of Australia to look out for include Victoria, South Australia (for the notable Barossa Valley and Coonawarra), Western Australia, home to the Margaret River district, and New South Wales, location of the Hunter Valley. The high-altitude vineyard area of Orange, the epicenter of the country's nineteenth-century gold rush, is today an emerging wine area literally on a higher level: two to three thousand feet.

NEW ZEALAND

This country's major wine stars are Sauvignon Blanc and Pinot Noir. European settlers planted the first vines here in the early 1800s, but it was only in the late twentieth century that New Zealand started producing distinctive, high-quality wines that won international notice and admiration. The country is the world's most southerly (and also among the coolest) wine regions—but that only makes it all the more appealing to New Zealand's adventurous vintners. Known for Sauvignon Blanc, New Zealand is appreciated for both its high quality and good value. In the Central Otago region, Pinot Noirs are fetching high prices and high praise. There are three main growing regions in new Zealand—Marlborough, Hawke's Bay, and Gisborne—and you'll find more than 300 wineries, many of them trendy, well-regarded boutiques.

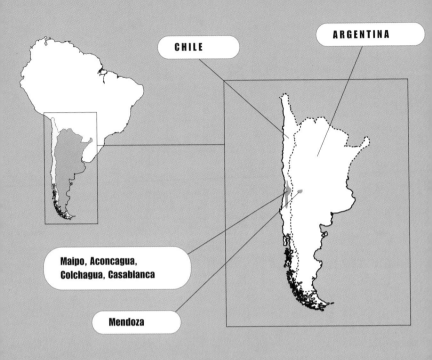

CHILE

ARGENTINA

Maipo, Aconcagua, Colchagua, Casablanca

Mendoza

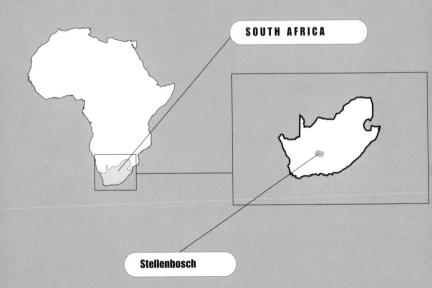

SOUTH AFRICA

Stellenbosch

SOUTH AMERICA AND SOUTH AFRICA

CHILE

Chile produces and sells wines around the world that range from luxury-class to extremely affordable, yet almost all are high-quality. Wine-producing regions to look for include Maipo, Aconcagua, Colchagua, and Casablanca. Some of the best grapes grown in Chile include Cabernet Franc, Syrah, Malbec, Merlot, and Carmenère, a hearty red wine. Bordeaux-style blends made from Cabernet Sauvignon, Merlot, and Cabernet Franc are also common.

ARGENTINA

Try Argentine Malbec. It is Argentina's strong suit, much of it grown in the high-altitude vineyards of Mendoza, a high desert region that forms the country's best wine-producing area. Malbec, a wine grape used to blend with others in Bordeaux, now stands largely on its own, though it is sometimes blended with Cabernet Sauvignon. Other wines worth trying include Syrah, Bonarda (similar to the Italian Barbera), Chardonnay, and Torrontes, a spicy Muscat-like grape native to Argentina and similar to Gewürztraminer.

SOUTH AFRICA

Look for Stellenbosch South African wine. This premier winemaking region is located outside coastal Cape Town and is fast gaining a reputation as a beautiful wine-country region to visit and a quality producer of elegant wines. Stellenbosch makes excellent wines from the Sauvignon Blanc grape in a crisp, lean style. Other wines include Chardonnay, Merlot, Cabernet Sauvignon, and a local red, Pinotage (a red grape cross of Pinot Noir and Cinsault). Pinotage wines from many Stellenbosch wineries are rapidly gaining international appeal.

what wine

10
talk means

Many people scoff at the esoteric or silly-sounding lingo wine experts use to describe wines, but the professionals defend their use of such language by saying that someone had to develop a set of terms to analyze and describe the taste sensations, feelings, and experiences that wine evokes in people. Both sides have a point. I don't go overboard on "wine-speak" when talking about wine. But it's often useful to borrow from the language used to describe food—so I might use words such as "spice," "chocolate," "apple," "cherry," "vanilla," "honey," and "coffee." This is because wine comprises more than 200 chemical compounds, many of which are identical or similar to those found in fruits, vegetables, spices, and herbs. Both wine and food leave flavors on the palate, and the same molecules that give bananas or chocolate their tastes show up in wine. This simple glossary explains all you need to know in a down-to-earth way.

Acidity

A wine's natural acids give it a crisp or tart taste. Natural acids in the wine grapes produce this crispness. Grapes, and thus wine, have three primary acids: tartaric, malic, and citric. Wine is described as high (or low) in acidity.

Aroma

Odor has a great deal to do with taste. Your nose can identify more than 2,000 different odors, while your tongue tastes just four main tastes: sweet, salty, bitter, and sour. There is a fifth taste the Japanese have discovered called *umami* that translates best as "savory". A wine's aroma is the smell of the wine; common descriptors for wine's aromas include "fruity," "floral," and "earthy." Technically, the aroma differs from its "bouquet" (see opposite).

Astringent

This is a tactile sensation, best described as the mouth-puckering feeling you get when drinking certain red wines. This drying sensation in the mouth comes from strong or young tannins.

Barrel-fermented

White wine fermented in an oak barrel instead of a stainless-steel tank. Chardonnays are often made this way, as are some Sauvignon Blancs. Stainless steel gives leaner, more austere flavors compared to the fuller flavors produced by oak fermentation.

Blanc de blancs (literally "white of whites")

Any wine made solely from white grapes. The term is usually applied to 100-percent Chardonnay, Champagne, or sparkling wine.

Blanc de noirs (literally "white of blacks")

A white or slightly tinted wine made from red grapes, such as Pinot Noir and Pinot

Meunier. The term is usually applied to Champagne or sparkling wine. The tint comes from the color pigments in the red grape skins.

Body

The weight or feeling of the wine on the palate, which can range from light to heavy or full.

Botrytis

Botrytis cinerea is a vine disease caused by a fungus that attacks the skin of grapes in warm, misty fall weather, effectively withering them and concentrating their juices. It is also known as "noble rot," and creates the basis for some of the best sweet and dessert wines.

Bouquet

Smells that derive from the winemaking, barrel-aging, and bottle-aging of a wine. This is different from what is meant by "aroma" (see opposite), which is the fruity, floral, or earthy, etc.

smells that the wine emits.

Buttery

Often used to describe white wines (particularly those that have been oak-aged—especially Chardonnay), this term indicates a rich, creamy aroma and flavor in a wine that usually comes from a winemaking process called "malolactic fermentation." If you like this flavor in a white wine, look for wines that say they have undergone this type of fermentation. This information may appear on the back label of the bottle.

Character

Term used to describe the distinct attributes of the grape variety used to make a wine. A Cabernet Sauvignon, a deep red wine, for instance, has a totally different character from a Riesling, which is a light white wine.

Chewy

A term that can cause much head-shaking and

bewildered looks when non-professionals come across it. It's often used to describe big, rich red wines and indicates a dense, deep, tannic wine that has a mouth-filling texture. You wouldn't actually chew it, of course, but you might experience a definite inclination to try!

Claret

British term for the classic red Bordeaux blend of Bordeaux, France. In other parts of the world it sometimes refers to a red table wine.

Clean

Used to describe a wine that lacks unpleasant aromas or tastes.

Closed

Term used to describe any wine that does not give off very much smell or taste. But you should make sure that it's not your cold or sinus condition that's causing the problem before you start blaming the wine!

If you're still sure the wine is "closed," try aging it and/or decanting it into another, more open, container to help open it up.

Complex

Complimentary term used for a wine that displays layered aromas, flavors, and texture. These multiple tastes or sensations could come from the quality of the grapes used, the winemaking techniques, or its development in the bottle after some time.

Cooked

People say a wine is cooked when it has been accidentally exposed to temperatures that are too high. A cooked wine is a spoiled wine.

Corked wine

A wine that is "off-tasting" and has been ruined by moldy smells from a bad cork. The fruitiness of the wine has been diminished and the smell and taste is often described as wet cardboard or wet newspapers. It is estimated that as many as 10 percent of wine bottles are "corked," a result of mold growing in the cork known as "cork taint." Cork, from the bark of cork trees grown in the western Mediterranean, is most often used to stop wine bottles because it is light, elastic, and impermeable to most liquids and gases. When a wine is "corked" or "corky," it is appropriate to reject the bottle in a restaurant or return it to a retail store.

Cuvée

Literally, wine contained in a *cuve*, or vat. The word has several meanings, including that of a blend. In Champagne and sparkling-wine production it can refer to wine made from a first pressing. In Burgundy, it is interchangeable with *cru*, or growth. It can also refer simply to a "lot" of wine.

Delicate

Used to describe a light, soft, fresh wine, usually a white wine. To call a red wine "delicate" would not be considered praise.

Dry

The opposite of sweet. This means the wine—whether red, white, rosé, or sparkling—has little or no sugar or sweetness in it. Almost all red table wines are dry, as are many white wines. A "fruity" wine can still be dry, since the term refers to fruit characteristics rather than sugar content. It is possible for the same grape variety, such as a Riesling, to be made in an off-dry, dry, or dessert-wine style. The longer the grapes ripen on the vines, the higher their final sugar content will be.

Earthy

Term often used to describe complex aromas and flavors detected in a wine, such as those of mushroom or earth.

Elegant

Yes, we'd all love to be described like this—and in fact, it's a term often used to describe a wine. Actually, it's a somewhat slippery usage, since, as with lots of things, what may be considered elegant to one person might not be to another. Generally, when using this word, wine experts are describing a well-balanced wine with a distinctive character.

Enologist

The American and South African spelling of oenologist: One who studies wine and winemaking.

Fining

The traditional method of clarifying wine by removing microscopic elements. This is usually achieved by using a fining agent, which could be activated carbon or charcoal, gelatin, clay (bentonite), or egg whites—even dried fish bladders (isinglass).

Finish

The final impression a wine makes in your mouth after being swallowed. It can range from short to long. Highest praise usually goes to wines with long finishes.

Firm

Used to describe the texture and structure of a wine, usually young, tannic reds, or wines with fairly high acidity.

Flabby/flat

A term used for characteristics of a wine lacking crisp acidity and a sturdy mouth-feel. You might use this word for a wine that has no particular structure or texture. Just as for people, this is not considered a compliment for a wine!

Fleshy

A word you might use to describe a wine that is fatter than a "meaty wine," but is also less vigorous and more smooth in texture.

Flinty

Often used to describe good Chablis; similar to a mineral tone.

Full-bodied

As opposed to "flabby" or "flat," this term is used to define a wine with a rich texture that fills the mouth and has a certain weight on the palate. This is a positive and complimentary attribute and means that you are likely to enjoy the wine.

Fruit-forward

Wine writers and other experts like to use this tasting term to describe a wine that has predominant fruit flavors—usually of the grapes used to make it, but also other fruit that you notice before you note other aspects of the wine, such as acidity or tannin.

Green

As with fruit, this term is used for wine when it shows unripe, excessively tart and sometimes harsh flavors and textures on the palate.

Hard

Similar to a "closed" wine (see page 146) and used when a wine has a texture and structure that does not allow you to taste any flavors.

Highly extracted

Sometimes wine writers will say that a wine is "highly extracted." What does this mean? Extract comprises the substances in a wine that constitute its body, flavor, and color. A highly extracted wine would be one with heavy extracts and would therefore be full-bodied, with concentrated flavors, and perhaps a dark and opaque color.

Hot

Used to describe a wine that has an excessively high alcohol content that "burns" the palate.

Lean

A wine often high in acidity, and lacking fruit flavors. Depending on what style wines you like, this could be considered praise, particularly for certain white wines, such as Sauvignon Blanc, Pinot Blanc, or Pinot Gris.

Legs

Term deriving from the long, thin lines of liquid visible inside a wine glass as it coats the glass and drips down its sides after you have swirled or tasted the wine.

Length

Refers to the finish of a wine. "Good length" means that the taste the wine leaves in the mouth lingers well after the wine has been swallowed.

Light-bodied

A wine that is delicate and pleasant, with light aromas, flavors, and texture.
A good Riesling might be light-bodied, but if a Cabernet Sauvignon were so described, this would indicate a criticism.

Lively

When someone describes a wine as "lively," it generally means that it is young, fruity, and has bright, vivacious flavors.

Malolactic fermentation

The conversion of hard, apple-type malic acid in wine to soft, milk-type lactic acid, which reduces the tart, green apple flavors and adds rich, buttery flavors. When a white wine is described as "creamy" or "buttery," it has probably gone through malolactic fermentation. This is a stylistic choice a winemaker makes. Some wines, such as many California Chardonnays, undergo this process, while others do not. It is also known as "ML."

Medium-bodied

Used to describe a wine with good weight and texture. It is less heavy than "full-bodied," but weightier than a wine that would be called "light."

Méthode champenoise

The traditional method of making French Champagne. The wine undergoes two fermentations, the second in the bottle, that creates natural carbonation and gives the wine its bubbles.

Mouth-feel

Term used to convey the impression or feel of wine in the mouth. This can be highly subjective, of course, especially when describing the tactile sensations such as "heat" from high alcohol content or "heaviness" of the liquid due to its density from high alcohol and sugar.

Must

Unfermented grape juice, as opposed to grape skins, pips, and stalks. Called "pomace" in the U.S., *marc* in France.

Non-vintage

Many Champagnes or sparkling wines are non-vintage, meaning they do not bear a vintage date. Many are *cuvées* (see page 147), or blends that contain wine from more than one vintage.

Oaky

Term used to describe the aromas and flavors contributed by oak barrels (or oak chips) during a wine's fermentation or aging. Oak lends such flavors or aromas as vanilla, caramel, smoke, spice, or toast (the inside of each barrel is "toasted" with fire in varying degrees).

Residual sugar

Technical term used to describe the amount of sugar left over in a wine after fermentation is complete. It varies widely among different types of wine. A dry table wine, such as a Cabernet Sauvignon you would drink with a steak, would have residual sugar as low as .1 or .2 percent. A dessert wine could have residual sugar as high as thirty percent.

Oxidation

When a wine is exposed to too much oxygen, it turns brownish and takes on a cooked or baked flavor like sherry. This can occur when the wine is badly stored at fluctuating temperatures, causing the wine to expand and contract and pushing the cork out. The corks loosen, exposing the wine in the bottles to oxygen. Very dry storage conditions may also cause high levels of exposure to oxygen by drying out the cork, which lets in air. An oxidized wine is spoiled.

Phylloxera

This tiny root-eating louse damages the leaves and roots of grapevines, and was responsible for killing more than three million acres of vines in Europe in the late nineteenth century. Grafting vines onto phylloxera-resistant rootstock is the only known way to combat this pest, and it was discovered in the late 1800s that native American vines were immune; hence most classic European vines were grafted onto American rootstock.

Round

A term used for a well-balanced wine showing smooth flavors and texture.

Sommelier

A butler, cellarman, or anyone in charge of wine. *Sommeliers* can also act as wine-buyers for a restaurant, and are highly educated about wine. Always ask their advice, as they can offer some good suggestions when you are not sure what to drink, or you are in the mood to try something new.

Sparkling wine

Term used for any wine that contains bubbles. The opposite of still wine. Sparkling wine is called Sekt in Germany, cava in Spain, and spumante and Prosecco in Italy.

Still wine

Any wine without bubbles.

aging

This French term indicates the wine has been aged "on its lees"—the term applied to dead yeast cells. The process results in greater complexity and creaminess of the finished wine. Wine not aged on its lees is clarified before aging.

Table wine

A simple, red, white, or rosé still wine served for day-to-day occasions.

Tannin

More often something you feel in your mouth rather than taste, but as a taste it's often bitter like the bitterness you detect in some teas or grape seeds. This is a major component of a red wine's structure and a natural preservative (this is also found in walnuts, and other foods). Tannins in wine come from grape skins, but they can also come from the oak barrels in which the wine is aged. Tannins need to be balanced with fruit; when they aren't, they leave a tactile sensation in the mouth felt in the middle of the tongue and sometimes described as "mouth-puckering." As a wine gets older, its tannins mellow. There is a greater tannin content in red wines than in white, which is why collectors age more red wines than white. The tannins help them develop over time.

Terroir

A French winemaking concept that refers to the combined effects of soil, climate, sun exposure in certain areas of vineyards, and other elements of grape-growing. It reflects the French belief that the specific place where grapes are grown is reflected in the taste of the wine. There is no exact translation in English, but winemakers in other parts of the world, such as California, also believe strongly that *terroir* is important.

Thin

Word used to describe a wine lacking in body and flavor. It usually describes an unpleasantly watery wine.

Toasting

What wine barrel-makers, or coopers, do when constructing a barrel. They heat the inside of the barrel to help the wood release flavors into the wine that will ferment in it. There can be a light, medium, or heavy toast in the barrel, which impacts on the flavors and aromas of the wine differently during aging.

Toasty

Usually describes a pleasant aroma in wine that comes from the "toasting" over fire of oak barrels in the process of barrel-making.

Varieties

Any grapes used to make wine. Some of the most popular varieties are Cabernet Sauvignon, Pinot Noir, Chardonnay, Sauvignon Blanc, and Riesling, but there are hundreds. A varietal wine is named by the dominant grape from which it's made, e.g. a Chardonnay or a Riesling.

Vintage

This is the year in which the wine grapes were harvested and fermented to make a wine. The vintage is important for almost all wines, since it refers to the weather conditions under which the grapes were grown. The bulk of Champagnes or sparkling wines are non-vintage because they are made from blends of different years.

Vintner

The owner of a winery and/or vineyards where wine grapes are grown. Vintner does not necessarily mean a winemaker (those who actually make the wine), though in smaller operations they may be one and the same.

Vintage chart

These charts rate vintage years for wine and advise you on what was "a good year" and what was not. They can be useful in deciding what to buy, order in a restaurant, or to age—and when to drink up.

Viticulture

The study, science, and practice of grape-growing.

Winemaker

The person who makes wine. He or she usually has a degree in enology or fermentation science, but some winemakers are self-taught or learn on the job. An important part of a winemaking education involves traveling to different high-quality wine regions of the world to work during their harvests and learn how grape-growing and winemaking are done in various climates and under different conditions.

Yeasty

This attribute in a wine suggests a pleasingly fresh, dough- or biscuit-like aroma and/or flavor.

INDEX